A BUSINESS CONSULTANT'S CASE DIARY

21 REAL CASES FROM MY CONSULTING JOURNEY

AR RANJITH

ISBN
Paperback 979-8-89777-922-2
Hardcase 979-8-89961-857-4

CONTENTS

Contents

PART 6

MARKETING & SALES PITFALLS

PART 7

LEADERSHIP & GROWTH CHALLENGES

Preface

Entrepreneurship is often romanticised as a thrilling journey of vision, passion, and hustle. But behind the scenes, the reality is different—cash flow nightmares, operational chaos, employee struggles, expansion missteps, and branding disasters. Over the years, I have had the opportunity to work closely with businesses across various industries, witnessing first-hand the challenges that entrepreneurs face and helping them find structured solutions.

This book is a collection of real experiences from my consulting journey—stories of businesses that struggled, adapted, and, in many cases, turned things around. The names, places, and people in these stories have been altered, but the core lessons remain untouched. Every case you read here is based on real businesses, real mistakes, and real solutions that I have worked on.

For entrepreneurs, this book serves as a mirror and a guide. You may see your own struggles reflected in these pages, and, more importantly, you will find insights on how to navigate them. The common thread running through these stories is the importance of systems—without them, businesses run on memory, emotions, and guesswork, often leading to unnecessary struggles. But when structured processes are put in place, growth becomes sustainable, and success is no longer left to chance.

Whether you are a first-time entrepreneur or a seasoned business owner, this book will give you a practical, no-nonsense perspective on what works and what doesn't in running a business. More than theories, this is about what actually happens on the ground—and how to fix it.

Let's dive into the world of business as it truly is—messy, unpredictable, but absolutely fixable with the right systems.

PART 1

LAYING THE FOUNDATION

1

THE ART OF BUYING RIGHT – WHEN PURCHASE BECOMES A PROFIT CENTRE

The Sweet Mess

Meet **Mohan**, a passionate entrepreneur and the proud owner of **Malabar Magic Sweets**, a confectionery business famous for its crispy banana chips, melt-in-your-mouth Mysore Pak, and rich cashew *burfis*.

He had built his brand with **hard work and an obsession for quality**. But his bank balance refused to grow no matter how much he sold. Every month, his accountant, **Ramesh**, would walk into his office with a nervous look, holding a financial report that looked more tragic than a soap opera.

"Sir, we had great sales this month!"

Mohan would smile.

"But sir... our profit margins are barely there."

Mohan's smile would disappear faster than a free plate of laddoos.

The Silent Profit Killer: Poor Purchase Management

Mohan's confusion was understandable. His sweets were selling, his customers were happy, and his cash register kept ringing. But then, where was all the money going?

When we stepped in to **audit his purchase process**, we quickly found the answer—bad purchasing decisions were quietly eating away at his profits.

His **Purchasing Manager, Shibu**, was a loyal and hardworking guy. But like many in his position, he believed his job was just about **placing orders, ensuring stock levels, and getting things "on time."** He had never considered purchasing **a strategic function** that could improve profitability.

Here's what we found:

1. **Bulk Buying Was Draining Cash Flow**

    ♦ Shibu took **pride in negotiating bulk discounts**. He believed that buying **huge quantities meant better deals**.

    ♦ But in reality, **excess stock was just lying in storage, eating up working capital and leading to wastage.**

2. **Supplier Loyalty Was Costing More**

    ♦ Mohan had been **buying from the same suppliers for years** without checking if their prices were competitive.

    ♦ The suppliers had **slowly increased rates,** knowing Mohan would never look elsewhere.

3. **No System to Track Wastage & Stock Rotation**

    ♦ Over 12% of **flour sacks and sugar bags** were **expiring** or getting **infested** due to poor stock management.

    ♦ There was **no real-time tracking of stock movement**, which meant **unnecessary reorders** were being made.

Mohan was **losing lakhs without realising it.**

Step 1: The Supplier Shake Up – Let's Talk Business

The first thing we did was **shake up his supply chain.**

Step 1.1: The Negotiation Challenge

- We **challenged Shibu** to get fresh quotes from at least **five alternative suppliers.**
- To his **surprise**, we found vendors offering **the same raw materials at 10-15% lower prices.**

Step 1.2: The Quality Test

- We took sugar, flour, and oil from the existing supplier and compared it to the new vendors.
- **Blind testing** with Mohan's chefs revealed **zero difference in quality.**
- The only difference? **The cost.**

Step 1.3: The Pricing War

- We returned to the old suppliers and allowed them **to match prices.**

- Suddenly, the **same "best price" suppliers were willing to drop their rates!**

Result?

🚀 **Mohan's purchasing cost dropped by 12% instantly!**

Step 2: Stop Overbuying – Only Buy What You Need

The next step was to **stop hoarding stock** as if it were gold.

We introduced:

Stock Movement Analysis – Identifying which ingredients were actually being used vs. overstocked.

Reorder Level System – Instead of buying in bulk, we set up **minimum and maximum stock levels.**

Wastage Tracking – Any expired or damaged raw material had to be **logged and reviewed** to avoid repeating the same mistakes.

Result?

Stock wastage dropped by 30% within 2 months.

Step 3: Turning Purchase into a Profit Centre

With the **right vendors**, smarter buying, and better stock management, purchasing was no longer an expense—it became a **profit generator.**

- Mohan finally **saw his margins increase by 9% within three months**—without selling a single extra piece of Mysore Pak!

His suppliers were **unhappy**. One even called, saying, "Mohanji, we've done business for so many years… this is unfair."

Mohan finally had the confidence to say:

"Business runs on numbers, not emotions."

Lessons for Entrepreneurs: Stop Losing Money on Bad Purchases

Mistake	Why It's a Problem	Solution
Buying in Bulk Without a Plan	Ties up cash and increases wastage.	Use **demand-based purchasing** and set **stock levels**
Sticking to the Same Suppliers	Prices keep increasing without competition.	Get **multiple quotes** and **negotiate regularly**.
No Waste Tracking	Expired or damaged stock = direct losses.	**Audit inventory weekly** and use **stock rotation systems**.
No Supplier Performance Tracking	Late deliveries and inconsistent quality affect the business.	Keep a **vendor scorecard** to track pricing, delivery time and quality.
No-Cost Benchmarking	Prices keep rising, and you never realise it.	Compare prices **every 3-6 months** with the market.

Final Thoughts: Profit Begins at Purchase

Most entrepreneurs focus only on **sales and marketing** to improve profits. But the truth is, **your first profit is made when you buy smart.**

By simply **fixing how they purchase**, Mohan turned his struggling business into a **leaner, more profitable** enterprise—**without increasing sales, hiring more people, or working extra hours.**

Now, with his new profits, Mohan has opened **two new outlets**. And guess what? He also negotiated the rent down by 15%!

Because once you **learn the art of buying correctly,** every deal becomes a profit-making opportunity.

2

SUPPLIER WOES – THE DRAMA OF DELAYED DELIVERIES

The Vanishing Supplier & The Furious Customers

Sandeep was the proud owner of **Elite Kitchens**, a mid-sized modular kitchen manufacturing business. He was a guy who loved **perfection, aesthetics, and customer satisfaction**. But what he didn't love?

"Where the hell are my materials?!"

This was the most common sentence heard in his office.

If you had walked into Elite Kitchens' factory six months ago, you would have seen:

+ **Half-finished kitchen cabinets** stacked in a corner, waiting for materials that never arrived.

+ **Customers calling every day**, asking when their kitchens would be ready.

✦ **Sandeep pulling his hair out** while making excuses on why their dream kitchens were delayed.

And the reason for all this? **A supplier named Mr Ramesh.**

The Supplier Who Took His Own Sweet Time

Mr Ramesh was the *exclusive supplier* of the **plywood, laminates and hardware** used for Sandeep's high-end modular kitchens.

He was a nice guy. Always polite. Always apologetic. But always, **ALWAYS late.**

His promises were legendary:

✦ **"Sir, I'll deliver by Friday."** (Didn't happen.)

✦ **"Just two more days."** (Still nothing.)

✦ **"The truck has left; it should be there by evening."** (The truck was *never* seen.)

Every time Sandeep followed up, there was a **new excuse:**

🚚 "The truck broke down."

☁ "Heavy rains in the supplier's city."

📦 "Stock issues at the warehouse."

💀 "The manager was on leave."

Sandeep, being the trusting businessman he was, kept believing him until **it nearly destroyed his business.**

The Real Cost of Delayed Deliveries

Every time materials arrived late:

1. **Manufacturing got delayed** → Orders piled up.

2. **Customers got angry** → Negative word-of-mouth spread.

3. **Payments got stuck** → No deliveries = No installations = No invoices raised.

4. **Employees got frustrated** → Workers had nothing to do, but salaries still had to be paid.

Sandeep's business was running, but it was **bleeding from all sides**.

And the worst part? His **competitors were eating his customers alive.**

How We Fixed the Supplier Drama

When we stepped in, the first thing we told Sandeep was:

"Your supplier should never control your business. You should control your supplier."

So, we did what most businesses *never* do—we audited his supplier's performance and became aggressive about enforcing accountability.

Here's what we did:

Step 1: The Supplier Report Card – Exposing the Truth

We went through 6 months of supplier records and **scored Mr Ramesh on three parameters:**

1. **On time Delivery Rate** ⧗ → **41% (Fail** ✗ **)**

2. **Accuracy of Orders (Correct quantity & quality)** 📦 → **76% (Average** 🤷‍♂️ **)**

3. **Response Time for Issues** 📞 → **32% (Disaster** 🔔 **)**

When we showed these numbers to Sandeep, his **jaw dropped.**

The supplier he had trusted blindly **failed him 59% of the time.**

Step 2: The Supplier Showdown – Breaking the Comfort Zone

We **called a meeting with Mr. Ramesh** and did what Sandeep had never done before—

We gave him a performance-based contract.

Here's what we put in it:

☑ **A fixed delivery schedule** – No more vague promises.

☑ **Late penalty charges** – Every day of delay = ₹5,000 **fine.**

☑ **Backup supplier clause** – If he failed twice, we would **start sourcing from other vendors.**

Mr. Ramesh was *shocked.*

"Sir, we've worked together for years... why this strictness?"

Because business isn't about friendship, it's about results.

Step 3: Always Have a Backup – Never Depend on One Supplier

We immediately **onboarded two backup suppliers.**

1. **One for plywood & laminates.**

2. **One for hardware fittings.**

So, the next time Mr Ramesh delayed a shipment?

We simply ordered from Supplier B instead of waiting.

And guess what?

🚀 Within 60 days, **on-time deliveries went up from 41% to 92%.**

🚀 Production delays **decreased from 14 days to 3 days.**

🚀 Customer complaints **dropped by 70%.**

Lessons for Entrepreneurs: How to Control Supplier Delays

Mistake	Why It's a Problem	Solution
Depending on **one** supplier	No alternative if they fail.	Always have **two or more suppliers.**
Not tracking delivery performance	You won't realise delays are hurting you.	Keep a **monthly supplier report.**

Mistake	Why It's a Problem	Solution
Not having written terms.	Verbal promises mean nothing.	Use **contracts with penalties** for delays.
Not negotiating better terms	The supplier has no pressure to improve.	Demand **commitment on timelines**.
Not setting backup options	Leaves your business at risk.	Have a **Plan B for critical supplies**.

Final Thoughts: Control Your Supply Chain, Control Your Profits

Sandeep went from **chasing suppliers** to **being in charge of them**.

With **on-time deliveries, he could complete kitchen installations faster, invoice customers sooner, and unlock stuck cash flow.**

His **reputation improved,** and he stopped losing customers to competitors.

And the best part? He now **had the confidence to say no to unreliable suppliers.**

The next time Mr Ramesh made an excuse?

Sandeep just smiled and said, **"No problem. I'll call my other supplier."**

3

THE INVENTORY NIGHTMARE – WHEN TOO MUCH STOCK KILLS CASH FLOW

How One Business Was Drowning in Stock but Still Had "Nothing Available" for Customers!

Meet "Stockpiler" Sanjay – The King of Useless Inventory

Sanjay owned **Trendy Threads**, a mid-sized clothing store that sold premium men's fashion.

His shop was beautiful – sleek wooden shelves, warm lighting, and rows of stylish shirts, jackets, and jeans.

But there was **one big problem**.

Every time a customer walked in and asked for something, the answer was **always the same**:

🏬 **Customer:** "Do you have slim-fit formal shirts in navy blue?"

😰 **Salesman:** "Uhh… no, sir. But we have it in yellow?"

Customer: "How about size 40 in black chinos?"

Salesman: "Umm… we only have size 44 left, sir."

It was a **mystery**.

Sanjay's warehouse was **bursting with stock**, but somehow, customers **never found what they wanted.**

And because of this, **his sales were dropping rapidly.**

The Inventory Black Hole – Where Did the Money Go?

When we first visited Trendy Threads, Sanjay was sitting in his office with a **worried look and a cup of cold coffee.**

"I don't understand," he sighed. **"We've spent over ₹50 lakhs on stock, yet customers always leave empty-handed!"**

So, we decided to **dig into his inventory records.**

Here's what we found:

1. **10,000+ unsold shirts**, but mostly in odd sizes like **XS or XXL**.

2. **Too many outdated styles**, because Sanjay kept buying what *he* liked instead of what *customers* wanted.

3. **Duplicate Stock** – He had **15 boxes of the same ugly floral shirt** that no one in their right mind would wear.

4. **Expensive items collecting dust** – Premium jackets worth ₹5,000+ were just **sitting there for months.**

5. **No system to track what was selling** – Everything was **bought randomly** without checking demand.

Basically, **he had a warehouse full of useless clothes, but nothing that customers actually wanted.**

The Real Cost of Holding Dead Stock

Having **too much useless stock** is just as bad as **not having stock.**

Here's what Sanjay was facing:

✗ **Blocked Cash Flow** – ₹50 lakhs stuck in slow-moving stock meant **no money to buy new designs.**

✗ **Storage Costs** – The rent for his warehouse was **₹1 lakh per month** just to keep stock that wasn't selling.

✗ **Missed Sales** – Customers **walked out without buying** because their size or style was unavailable.

✗ **Discount Desperation** – Every 3 months, he had to sell old stock at a **70% discount** just to clear space.

His business wasn't growing – it was **suffocating under piles of dead inventory.**

How We Fixed the Inventory Disaster

Step 1: The 'Red Tag' System – Identifying Useless Stock

We walked through the warehouse with Sanjay's sales team and marked:

⬤ **Red Tag** – Stock that hadn't sold in 6 months.

◯ **Yellow Tag** – Slow-moving stock (selling fewer than 3 pieces per month).

◉ **Green Tag** – Fast-moving stock (selling regularly).

When we were done, **60% of his inventory had red tags!**

That meant **₹30 lakhs' worth of stock was just sitting there like a museum collection.**

Step 2: Clearing the Dead Stock – The 'Festival Sale' Trick

To **free up cash**, we didn't do a boring discount sale.

Instead, we launched **the limited-time "Flash Festival Sale"** with this marketing twist:

🔥 **Buy 2, Get 1 Free!** (Made customers buy more.)

🔥 **Exclusive VIP Preview for Regular Customers!** (Creating urgency.)

🔥 **Influencer Collab – "Style Your Look" Sessions** (Drove footfall.)

In just **15 days**, we cleared ₹22 **lakhs of dead stock** and recovered cash.

Step 3: Fixing the Buying Strategy – No More Guesswork

Sanjay's biggest mistake? **He was buying stock based on customer demand** instead of **his personal taste.**

So, we introduced a simple **3-step Buying System:**

📊 **Step 1: Weekly Sales Report** – Identify **top-selling and slow-moving items.**

👂 **Step 2: Customer Requests** – Track what customers are **asking for.**

🗃 **Step 3: Order Only What Sells** – No more bulk buying of random styles.

Step 4: Implementing the 'Never Out of Stock' Rule

Customers hate hearing, **"Sorry, we don't have your size."**

So, we set up a **Smart Replenishment System:**

✅ **Always keep the top 20% best-selling items in stock.**

✅ **Auto-reorder when the stock falls below 5 pieces per size.**

✅ **Stop ordering slow-moving items completely.**

The Turnaround – From Inventory Mess to Smart Stocking

💰 **Cash flow improved** – ₹22 lakhs of dead stock was converted into **fresh cash.**

⬊ **Storage costs dropped** – No more wasting ₹1 lakh per month on unnecessary warehousing.

☑ **Sales increased by 35%** – because customers actually found what they wanted.

◎ **Faster inventory turnover** – Now, 80% of the stock was sold **within 60 days** instead of sitting for months.

Sanjay no longer **guessed** what to buy. He used **data** to make decisions.

When customers walked in, they **found exactly what they were looking for.**

And the best part?

Sanjay stopped hoarding **ugly floral shirts.** 😂

Lessons for Entrepreneurs: How to Avoid the Inventory Trap

Mistake	Why It's a Problem	Solution
Stocking **randomly**	Leads to **dead stock and wasted money.**	Track **customer demand and sales trends**
No inventory tracking.	No idea what's selling or not.	Use **weekly reports** to monitor stock.
Overbuying slow-moving items.	Cash gets stuck in unsellable products.	Use the **Red-Yellow-Green Tag system.**

Mistake	Why It's a Problem	Solution
No strategy for clearance.	Stuck with outdated stock.	Run **Flash Sales & Bundle Offers.**
No auto-replenishment.	Customers don't find what they need.	Set a **minimum stock level for best sellers.**

Final Thoughts: Smart Inventory = More Profits

Sanjay went from **drowning in stock** to **running a lean and profitable inventory system.**

With **real-time tracking, smart purchasing, and better cash flow**, he **doubled his profits in just 4 months.**

Now, instead of **discounting his way to survival,** he's **selling what customers want** – at full price!

And the next time someone asks, "**Do you have this in size 40?**"

The answer is a confident "**YES, we do!**"

Instead of **chasing customers for payments,** they were **paying him on time—without excuses!**

And best of all? **His employees finally got their salaries on time.**

PART 2

INVENTORY & LOGISTICS CHALLENGES

4

THE WAREHOUSE MAZE – HOW ONE BUSINESS LOST LAKHS IN A MESSY STORE

The Chaos Begins

Meet Ramesh, a seasoned businessman from **Middle Kerala** who owned a bustling wholesale distribution company. His warehouse was legendary—not for its efficiency but sheer madness. It was where **inventory disappeared into a black hole**, staff embarked on treasure hunts to find products, and misplaced goods sometimes resurfaced months later—after they were no longer needed.

Ramesh had a simple philosophy for years: "If we have it, we'll sell it eventually." But reality hit hard when his accountant revealed that he had lost ₹25 lakhs in missing, expired, and unsellable inventory in just one year.

The Problems

1. **The Bermuda Triangle of Goods**

   + Products would arrive but never get logged into the system properly.

   + Staff had no idea where things were kept, leading to hours wasted searching.

   + Customers often cancelled orders because deliveries took too long.

2. **Dust, Decay, and Dead Stock**

   + Items that should have been sold first (FIFO method) were forgotten at the back of the warehouse.

   + Some products expired while sitting on the shelves.

   + Others were damaged due to poor storage conditions.

3. **Wrong Orders, Wrong Deliveries**

   + Invoices never matched the actual stock.

   + Customers frequently received the wrong items, causing returns and refunds.

   + Vendors got frustrated with repeated reorders of available things that were just **missing in the mess.**

The Fix

We took a **four-step approach** to turn the warehouse from a chaotic labyrinth into a well-oiled machine.

1. **Barcode Everything!** 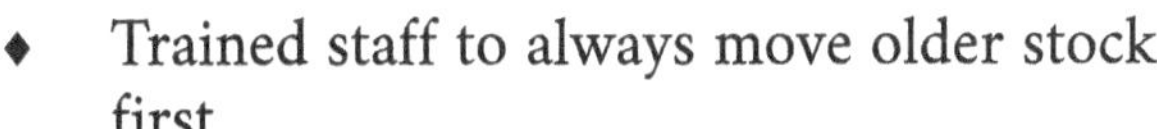

    ♦ Introduced a simple barcode and scanning system.

    ♦ Every product was scanned in and out, ensuring real-time stock updates.

    ♦ Result: **Search time reduced from 45 minutes per item to under 5 minutes.**

2. **Rearrange the Warehouse Like a Supermarket**

    ♦ Categorised and labelled sections clearly.

    ♦ High-moving products were kept near dispatch areas for quick access.

    ♦ Dead stock was identified and either liquidated or repositioned.

    ♦ Result: **Stocking errors dropped by 80%.**

3. **Implement FIFO & Regular Audits**

    ♦ Trained staff to always move older stock first.

    ♦ Monthly audits ensured that no item was forgotten.

    ♦ Result: **Expired stock loss reduced from ₹25 lakhs to just ₹3 lakhs.**

4. **Automate Reordering & Reporting**

    ♦ Integrated inventory software that alerted when stocks were low.

    ♦ Set up weekly reports to track slow-moving items.

- Result: **Stockouts were reduced by 60%, and overstocking was eliminated.**

The Results

In **six months**, Ramesh's business transformed:

Problem	Loss Before (₹)	After Fix (₹)
Lost inventory and misplacement	25,00,000	3,00,000
Expired and damaged goods	7,00,000	50,000
Order processing time	45 mins/item	5 mins/item
Stockouts and delivery delays	Frequent	Rare

The Lesson

A **warehouse is not just a storage space; if managed well, it can be a profit centre.** Ramesh's story proves that a messy store isn't just an inconvenience—it's a direct attack on your bottom line.

So, if your warehouse looks like a **junkyard rather than a business asset**, it's time to clean up, organise, and let technology do some heavy lifting.

Who knew **fixing a warehouse could make you laugh (and save lakhs)?**

5

The Phantom Stock – When Your System Says Yes but Shelves Say No

The Mysterious Case of the Missing Inventory

Manoj was convinced he had the perfect inventory system. His retail business in central Kerala ran on sophisticated software that tracked every item with "absolute precision." Or so he thought. The reality? His store's stock levels had all the accuracy of a weather forecast during the monsoon season—completely unreliable. On paper, his warehouse was overflowing. Customers were walking out empty-handed because the shelves were as bare as a temple on a weekday afternoon.

Things came to a breaking point when a customer walked in, eager to buy a high-end home appliance. The system confidently declared, "12 pieces in stock." But when the staff went to fetch one, they found... nothing. Nada. Zilch. The product had seemingly **evaporated into thin air**. This wasn't a one-time error—it was happening across multiple products. And every time it did, Manoj lost a sale, a customer, and some sanity.

Step 1: Diagnosing the Disaster

We started with a simple question: **Where was the stock going?**

After digging into months of records and warehouse checks, we uncovered three major problems:

1. **Over-Optimistic Data Entry**—Items were marked as "in stock" the moment they were ordered rather than when they actually arrived. So, in the system, they existed. In reality, they were still in a truck somewhere between Bengaluru and Kerala.

2. **Phantom Returns** – Customers who returned products were refunded, but the system never returned the items to inventory. Effectively, these products became **warehouse ghosts**—paid for but never resold.

3. **Shelf Shuffle Syndrome** – To make space, employees were **hiding slow-moving stock behind fast-moving items**. A rare species of toaster was found chilling behind a wall of blenders.

Step 2: Fixing the Mess

To bring the **phantom stock** back to reality, we took some drastic but effective measures:

✅ **Barcode System Upgrade** – We implemented **real-time barcode scanning** to ensure stock was counted when it entered the store, not just when it was ordered. This **cut down stock mismatches by 80%** within a month.

✅ **Shelf Audits with Incentives** – Employees were given a small **reward per correctly counted product**. Suddenly, even the most uninterested staff members turned into detectives, hunting down misplaced stock.

✅ **Customer Return System Overhaul** – We ensured **every return went through a quality check and was restocked immediately**. This alone **recovered ₹2.5 lakhs worth of lost inventory** within two months.

✅ **Weekly "Stock Reality Check"** – We introduced a physical stock check every Saturday instead of relying entirely on software. A simple count of high-value products **reduced mismatches by 90%**.

The Result: Profits Recovered, Sanity Restored

With these changes, Manoj's business saw a **20% increase in sales fulfilment** within the next quarter. More importantly, **customer complaints about "out of stock" items dropped by 70%**.

At the end of our project, I asked Manoj how he felt about his new system. His response?

"It's like finding out half my employees were imaginary friends I didn't know I had."

Lesson for Entrepreneurs: Don't trust your system blindly. Stock exists when you can physically see it, not just because a computer tells you so!

Summary Table: Fixing the Phantom Stock Problem

Issue	Impact	Solution	Result
Stock shown in the system but missing in reality.	Lost sales and customer frustration.	Introduced **barcode-based real-time tracking**.	Stock mismatches dropped by 80%.
Returns processed but not restocked.	Money lost on refunds without reselling.	Ensured **returns were quality checked and added back**	₹2.5 million worth of stock recovered.
Misplaced products in the warehouse.	Stock became "invisible" to the sales team.	Conducted **weekly audits** and gave **staff incentives**.	90% reduction in mismatches.
Over-optimistic data entry.	Inventory data was unreliable.	Delayed stock entry until **physically received.**	Accurate stock reports.

Want to avoid your stock turning into **warehouse ghosts? Start counting the real, not the virtual!**

6

JUST-IN-TIME OR JUST-IN-TROUBLE? – THE PERILS OF OVER-OPTIMISATION

The Great Bakery Blunder – When JIT Almost Killed a Business

Rahul owned a **chain of bakeries** in **South Kerala**, known for its **hot, crispy puffs and melt-in-the-mouth cakes.** Business was booming, but Rahul wanted to **increase profitability by reducing waste.**

He had just read an article on **"Just-in-Time"** **inventory management,** where a business **only orders ingredients exactly when needed**—so no money is wasted on extra stock.

"Brilliant!" Rahul thought. *"Why keep bags of flour sitting in my store when I can order them fresh daily?"*

So, he **reduced stock levels, trained his team on "lean operations," and ensured suppliers delivered exactly what was required**—nothing more, nothing less.

What could possibly go wrong?

The Day Everything Went Wrong

One morning, Rahul's bakery was **packed with customers.** The usual morning rush of office-goers was **double the size**, thanks to a viral social media post about his legendary egg puffs.

Perfect time for business, right?

However, the **bakery ran out of eggs.**

Yes, eggs. What you **need** to make puffs, cakes, and everything Rahul's bakery was known for.

"No problem," thought Rahul. *"Our supplier delivers fresh stock every morning. He should be here in five minutes."*

But today, **the supplier's van broke down** on the highway.

Delivery was delayed by three hours.

When the eggs arrived, **customers had left, orders were cancelled, and online reviews were brutal.**

The Aftermath: JIT vs. Reality

Rahul lost ₹75,000 **in a single day** because of **one missing ingredient.**

And because customers were disappointed, they started **buying from a competitor down the street.**

When we analysed his numbers, we found that:

📌 **His bakery was wasting just ₹8,000 worth of stock per month before JIT.**

📌 **But after JIT, a single delivery delay wiped out almost ten times that amount.**

📌 He lost 15% of his regular customers to competitors.

Rahul had **optimised his inventory so much that it became a time bomb.**

How We Fixed It

We needed to **fix this mess without bringing back unnecessary waste.** So, we made some **realistic adjustments** to his JIT approach:

✅ **Critical Stock Buffer:** We identified **10 key ingredients** (like eggs, flour, and butter) that should **always** have **at least 2 stock days.**

✅ **Supplier Backup Plan:** Instead of relying on **one supplier**, Rahul **found another local supplier** for emergencies.

✅ **Demand Forecasting:** We **analysed daily sales data** and pre-ordered stock based on past trends **instead of blindly ordering the same amount every day.**

✅ **Order Flexibility:** Instead of **daily strict orders,** we allowed some **wiggle room** for urgent needs—so staff could buy essentials from local markets in an emergency.

The Turnaround: Business Bounced Back

With these small but effective changes:

📌 **Stockouts reduced by 90%.**

📌 **Sales increased by ₹2 lakh in the next three months.**

📌 **Customer complaints dropped, and online ratings improved.**

Rahul still followed a **lean inventory model**, but it wasn't so lean this time **that it starved the business.**

His final verdict?

"JIT is great in theory, but in business, you don't gamble with eggs."

Summary Table: The Smart JIT Fix

Problem	Impact	Solution	Result
Ran out of eggs due to just-in-time (JIT).	₹75,000 lost in a day.	Kept **2 days' worth of buffer stock.**	**90% fewer stockouts**
Supplier delay = no backup plan.	Customers left for competitors.	Found a **second local supplier**.	Avoided future delivery issues.
Orders weren't based on demand.	Over-optimisation led to losses.	Used **past sales data for accurate ordering**.	₹2 lakh increase in sales.
No flexibility in purchasing.	Staff couldn't buy urgent items.	Allowed local emergency purchases.	Faster response during shortages.

Lesson for Entrepreneurs

JIT **isn't bad**—but **blindly following it without common sense can be a disaster.** If you're dealing with **fast-moving perishable goods, critical raw materials, or** seasonal demand, a little extra stock can save a LOT of money.

Because at the end of the day, **customers don't care about your efficiency – they just want their egg puffs.**

PART 3

ACCOUNTS & FINANCE NIGHTMARES

7

THE ACCOUNTS CATASTROPHE – WHEN PROFITS LOOK GREAT ON PAPER BUT THERE'S NO MONEY IN THE BANK!

How a ₹50 Crore Business Was Making Sales but Still Couldn't Pay Its Bills!

Meet "Broke" Balakrishnan – The Big Player with an Empty Wallet

Balakrishnan (Bala) was the proud owner of EverFresh Foods, a massive packaged snacks company. His business was a big name in Kerala – his banana chips, masala peanuts, and cashew brittle were sold across 800+ supermarkets and retail stores.

The numbers looked fantastic:

- Two fully operational factories
- 200+ distributors handling his products
- 500 tonnes of snacks produced every month
- Annual revenue of ₹50 Crores

Sounds great, right? Wrong.

Despite all this success, Bala had a big problem.

His bank balance was close to zero.

His staff salaries were being delayed.

His suppliers were threatening to stop deliveries.

His factory rent was due.

How could a ₹50 crore business be broke? 

The "Paper Profit" Illusion – Why He Was Stuck in a Cash Crunch

When I met Bala, he looked like a man who had just survived a storm. Messy hair, dark circles, and a half-finished cup of tea had gone cold.

"I don't understand," he groaned. "We're selling more than ever, but I have no money in my account!"

So, we pulled up his accounts.

Here's what we found:

1. Profits Were Just an Illusion – The "Outstanding" Problem

    ♦   80% of sales were on credit.

    ♦   Supermarkets and distributors took stock but paid only after 90–120 days.

    ♦   ₹15 Crores were "stuck" in receivables—money owed by retailers but not yet paid.

    So, while the company looked profitable *on paper*, there was no actual cash flow.

2. **Wrong Customers – The "Late Payers" List**

   ♦ 60% of his credit sales went to 5 large supermarkets—the same ones that always delayed payments.

   ♦ Some distributors hadn't paid him in over 6 months, yet he was still sending them more stock!

   ♦ No proper tracking of who owed what and by when.

3. **Spending Like a King – High Expenses, Low Control**

   ♦ Bala had 40 company vehicles, even though only 25 were needed.

   ♦ A new ₹2 Crore office renovation was underway while salaries were getting delayed.

   ♦ A fancy ₹15 Lakh billboard was set up, but suppliers were still unpaid.

The Cost of "Paper Profits" – How It Was Killing His Business

✗ Business looked profitable, but there was no money to run operations.

✗ Late payments led to a chain reaction – suppliers refused to provide raw materials on credit.

✗ Loans were piling up – paying interest instead of growing the business.

✖ Employee morale was dropping – salaries were delayed for months.

Bala's company was a classic example of "growth without control" – huge sales but even bigger problems.

How We Fixed the Accounts Disaster

Step 1: The "Red List" – Cutting Off the Worst Payers

We made a list of the worst customers—distributors and supermarkets who took stock but paid only after 6 months.

Then we took a bold step:

🚫 We stopped giving them stock until past dues were cleared.

🚀 Instead, we focused on smaller, high-paying customers who cleared bills in 30 days.

This alone freed up ₹3 million in 45 days!

Step 2: The "Cash-First" Model – Reducing Credit Dependence

Instead of blindly giving stock on credit, we introduced:

✔ Upfront Payment Discounts – Any distributor who paid in advance received an extra 2% discount.

✔ Shorter Credit Periods – From 120 days, we have reduced it to a maximum of 45 days.

✔ Penalty for Late Payments – Retailers who paid late had to pay an additional 2% after 60 days.

Result?

Distributors paid faster to avoid extra charges.

Step 3: Expense Control – The "Do We Really Need This?" Test

We ran a brutal cost-cutting audit.

▼ Sold 15 company vehicles – Only kept the ones truly needed.

▼ Stopped the office renovation – Because fancy interiors don't pay the bills!

▼ Cut wasteful marketing – No more ₹15 lakh billboards; switched to cheaper digital ads.

💰 Savings: ₹4 Crores in unnecessary expenses!

Step 4: Payment Tracking – No More Guessing Who Owes What

We introduced a simple payment tracking system:

📊 Weekly Reports – A clear dashboard showing who still owed money and for how long.

📞 Follow-Up Calls – Automated reminders to distributors 15 days before payment was due.

💳 Payment Links for Faster Collection – Instead of waiting, we started collecting payments online instantly.

This cut down outstanding payments by 40% in just 3 months!

The Turnaround – From Broke to Cash-Positive in 6 Months

☑ Bank balance went from ₹5 Lakhs to ₹4 Crores – thanks to faster payments.

☑ Distributors paid quicker – average payment time dropped from 120 to 45 days.

☑ Expense control led to higher profits – cutting unnecessary costs added ₹4 million to net profits.

☑ No more salary delays – employees got paid on time, boosting productivity.

For the first time in two years, Bala had money in his account!

Lessons for Entrepreneurs: How to Avoid the Accounts Trap

Mistake	Why It's a Problem	Solution.
Selling too much on credit	Business looks profitable, but cash flow is suffering	Keep the credit period short and reward upfront payments.
Not tracking outstanding payments	Money gets stuck with slow-paying customers	Use weekly payment tracking and reminders.

Mistake	Why It's a Problem	Solution.
Relying on a few significant customers	Big buyers delay payments, causing cash shortages	Focus on smaller, faster-paying customers.
Spending Money Before Earning	Cash gets wasted on fancy offices and ads	Cut unnecessary expenses and prioritise payments.
Not penalising late payments	Customers take advantage and delay payments even more	Charge late fees and offer early payment discounts.

Final Thoughts: Cash Flow is King!

Bala's story is a reminder that sales don't matter if money isn't coming in.

By focusing on cash flow instead of just revenue, he turned his broke ₹50 Crore business into a cash-positive company.

8

THE TEXTILE EMPIRE THAT SOLD EVERYTHING... EXCEPT PROFITS!

How We Turned a Messy Fashion Store into a Profit Machine!

If you want to see pure **retail chaos**, visit a large textile store on a festival weekend. People fighting over the last red saree, salesmen sprinting between shelves, kids playing hide-and-seek under clothing racks—it's **a mix of a battlefield and a wedding house.**

And right in the middle of all this madness was **Thomas Chettan**, the owner of *Royal Silks,* standing helplessly near the billing counter.

💬 *"Ningal onnum parayanda... Business nannayi pokunnu! Paksha paisa evide poyaa?"*

Translation: *"Business is doing well! But where is the money going?"*

That's a classic Kerala businessman problem. **Sales? High. Customers? Happy. Profits? Missing.**

So, we did what we do best—we **walked in, dug into the mess, and fixed it.**

Step 1: Finding Where the Money Was Leaking

We didn't need to check the books to find the first problem.

1. **The Warehouse Was a Textile Graveyard**

    Behind the main showroom was a **storehouse full of unsold stock—some clothes were so old they could be classified as antiques.** Staff had no clue what was inside, and new stock kept coming in while the old stock kept sitting.

    🔖 *Problem:* **Money was stuck in unsold inventory.**

2. **Discounts Were Decided Based on Mood**

    Salesmen gave discounts randomly just to close a sale. One customer got a churidar for ₹1,500, and another got the same one for ₹1,100—just because the salesman liked their bargaining skills.

    🔖 *Problem:* **Uncontrolled pricing was affecting profit margins.**

3. **Staff Was Functioning Like a Government Office**

    -   No incentive to sell more.

    -   Billing took forever.

    -   Some staff were more interested in gossip than customers.

💼 *Problem:* **Slow sales + poor customer service = Lost business.**

Step 2: Fixing the Textile Circus

1. **"Operation Clean Up": Clearing the Warehouse Mess**

    📌 **We ran a "Mega Clearance Sale"** and eliminated old stock by offering big discounts (but still making a profit).

    📌 **Started a barcode system** so the stock could be tracked properly.

    📌 **Only ordered based on sales data** instead of blindly buying new stock.

    ✅ **Result:** Warehouse **freed up space and recovered ₹3 Crores in blocked money.**

2. **"Discount Discipline": No More Random Price Cuts**

    📌 **Standardised pricing** – fixed profit margins on all items.

    📌 **No unapproved discounts** – salesmen could only apply discounts during specific promotions.

    📌 **Premium pricing**—branded sarees & wedding collections got **higher margins** than unnecessary discounts.

    ✅ **Result: Profit margins increased by 12% without affecting sales.**

3. **"Customer First" Training for Staff**

    📌 **Introduced an incentive system** – salespeople now had **targets** and bonuses for better performance.

⚡ **Billing speed improved** – cashiers were trained to **complete a bill in under 5 minutes.**

⚡ **Customer service focus**—staff were taught to sell smartly, not just push random products.

☑ **Result:** Customers spent **less time waiting and more time buying.**

Step 3: The Bigger Game Plan

After fixing the basics, we planned long-term strategies:

🚀 **Started an online store** to sell directly across Kerala.

🚀 **Launched a loyalty programme** – customers earned points and returned for more.

🚀 **Opened new stores in a controlled manner** (without making the same mistakes).

6 Months Later: The Transformation!

✔ **Dead stock reduced by ₹3 crores**

✔ **Profits increased from 6% to 18%.**

✔ **Customer complaints dropped by 50%.**

✔ **Staff efficiency improved significantly**

And Thomas *Chettan?* **Finally smiling.**

💬 *"Ithrem paisa namukkundayirunnille? Enthokkeyo nadannittu karyam manasilayi!"*

(*"Have we always had this much money? After so much struggle, I finally understand!"*)

Key Takeaways for Business Owners

Problem	Old Situation	New Solution
Inventory	Warehouse full of unsold stock	Barcode system and demand-based stocking
Pricing	Random discounts based on negotiation	Fixed profit margins and structured pricing
Sales Staff	No motivation, lazy billing	Incentives and faster customer service
Growth Strategy	Expansion without profit control	Smart scaling and online sales

Final Thought: Sales Don't Matter if Profits Are Missing!

Most big businesses focus on *"How much are we selling?"* but never on *"How much are we actually making?"*

Fixing **inventory, pricing, and staff performance** turned *Royal Silks* into a **real money-making business.**

9

Tax Troubles – The Case of a Business Almost Drowned by GST

Introduction: A Storm Brewing

Raghav was a proud IT services business owner, successfully running his company and managing steady growth. He had registered for GST when it was introduced, but he saw it as just another compliance formality like many entrepreneurs. He treated tax filing as an occasional task rather than a structured process.

He was lax about timely submissions for the first few months, assuming minor delays wouldn't be an issue. But as time passed, penalties accumulated, cash flow started drying up, and his clients began withholding payments due to mismatches in filings. Raghav realised he was in serious trouble when the tax authorities sent a hefty notice detailing unpaid dues and fines.

The Real Problems Uncovered

As we analysed Raghav's finances, the underlying issues became clear:

- ✦ **Missed Filing Deadlines** – Delays in monthly GST returns led to a cumulative penalty of ₹3.5 lakhs over 18 months.

- ✦ **Incorrect Input Tax Credit (ITC) Claims** – Mismatched invoices meant ₹12 lakhs in ITC remained unclaimed, straining working capital.

- ✦ **Cash Flow Disruptions** – Sudden bulk tax payments without planning led to operational cash shortages.

- ✦ **Client Non-Compliance** – Some clients had not filed their GST correctly, delaying payments and causing further financial strain.

- ✦ **Lack of Internal Control** – No system was in place to track GST filings, payments, or reconciliation with service invoices.

The Rescue Plan

To rescue Raghav from this financial crisis, we implemented a structured recovery plan:

1. **Penalty Negotiation & Compliance Correction** – We filed for penalty waivers, reducing fines by 40% and set up backdated returns.

2. **ITC Recovery Strategy** – An in-depth audit of past invoices helped reclaim ₹9 lakhs in unclaimed ITC.

3. **Automated Filing System** – A cloud-based GST software with real-time reconciliation was introduced for timely filings.

4. **Cash Flow Optimisation** – GST liabilities were spread into manageable monthly allocations instead of bulk tax payments.

5. **Client Coordination** – Clients were guided on proper GST filing, ensuring no further payment delays.

6. **Team Training & Process Implementation** – Staff received training on compliance, preventing future lapses.

The Impact of the Solutions

Within six months, the transformation was evident:

+ **Reduced Penalties:** ₹1.4 lakhs saved through successful appeals and timely corrections.

+ **Recovered ITC:** ₹9 lakhs reclaimed, significantly improving liquidity.

+ **Steady Cash Flow:** A structured approach prevented future tax shocks.

+ **Seamless Compliance:** No more missed deadlines, avoiding unnecessary stress and legal issues.

Lessons for Entrepreneurs

Mistake	Lesson Learned
Delaying GST filings	Even a small delay can snowball into significant penalties. Automate and file on time.
Ignoring ITC mismatches	Regular reconciliation ensures maximum tax savings. Don't leave money unclaimed.
Poor cash flow planning	Set aside GST funds monthly to avoid financial strain.
Relying on non-compliant clients	Ensure clients file their GST correctly to avoid payment delays.
No internal tax tracking	Implement a structured system to monitor filings, payments, and reconciliations.

Conclusion

Raghav's experience is a cautionary tale for entrepreneurs who take tax compliance lightly. While GST can feel like a burden, managing it well can actually improve financial health. Today, Raghav not only files his GST like clockwork but also advises fellow business owners on staying ahead of tax troubles.

After all, GST doesn't have to stand for "Generally Stressful Transactions" – as long as you stay prepared!

PART 4

HR & TEAM MANAGEMENT BLUNDERS

10

HIRING HUSTLES – THE 'PERFECT EMPLOYEE' MYTH THAT ALMOST KILLED A STARTUP

Introduction: The Never-Ending Search for the "Perfect" Team

Amit had a dream – a tech startup that would revolutionise workflow automation for small businesses. He had the vision, the funding, and the first wave of clients ready. But one problem was **he couldn't find the "right" employees.**

Every candidate he interviewed was missing something. Some were too expensive, some lacked startup experience, and some didn't seem "passionate" enough. Months passed, and instead of building his product, Amit was stuck in an endless hiring loop. The workload piled up, deadlines were missed, and frustration set in.

💬 "Good employees are impossible to find! Maybe I should just do everything myself?"

That's when we stepped in.

Step 1: Diagnosing the Hiring Mess

A quick analysis of Amit's hiring approach revealed some serious problems:

1. **The Myth of the "Perfect" Employee**

   Amit wanted someone who was:

   ✔ Highly skilled in tech **and** business

   ✔ Willing to work startup hours **but** at a low salary.

   ✔ Passionate about the product **and** okay with chaos.

   ✔ Self-driven **yet** willing to take constant instructions

   🔒 **Problem:** He was looking for a unicorn that didn't exist.

2. **Overcomplicated Hiring Process**

   Amit was conducting **5 rounds** of interviews, including a written test, a case study, and even a personality evaluation—before even discussing salary!

   🔒 **Problem:** Good candidates lost patience and took jobs elsewhere.

3. **Hiring Without a Retention Plan**

   Even after making a few hires, people left within **weeks.** They weren't aligned with the company's expectations and felt lost.

🔒 **Problem:** High churn rate has led to wasted hiring efforts.

Step 2: Fixing the Hiring Chaos

Once we identified the issues, we implemented a structured hiring and retention strategy:

1. **Redefining the "Right" Employee**

   📌 Instead of searching for a unicorn, we **prioritised skills that mattered.**

   📌 We **divided roles into core skills versus trainable skills**—hiring for must-have abilities and training for the rest.

   📌 Hired a mix of **experienced professionals** (for stability) and **freshers** (for energy and adaptability).

   ✅ **Result:** The hiring process became more realistic and faster.

2. **Speeding Up the Hiring Process**

   📌 Reduced interview rounds from **5 to 2** – a practical skill test followed by a direct discussion.

   📌 Salary and expectations were discussed **upfront** to avoid last-minute surprises.

   📌 Offered trial-based contracts to uncertain candidates instead of rejecting them outright.

   ✅ **Result:** Time-to-hire was reduced by 60%, and fewer candidates dropped out mid-process.

3. **Retention Plan from Day One**

📌 Structured **onboarding & training** to help new employees settle in quickly.

📌 Defined **clear career growth paths** within the company to improve motivation.

📌 Created a **flexible yet structured work culture**—balancing startup energy with stability.

✅ **Result:** Employee satisfaction increased, and early attrition significantly decreased.

Step 3: The Bigger Game Plan

Once the hiring process was streamlined, we helped Amit plan for long-term stability:

🚀 **Introduced referral hiring** – New employees brought in candidates who fit the culture.

🚀 **Launched an internship programme**—A fresh talent pipeline that could be trained and hired.

🚀 **Created performance-based incentives** – Employees now had a reason to stay and grow.

6 Months Later: The Transformation!

✔ Hired **8 solid employees** without unnecessary delays.

✔ Reduced **early attrition** from 60% to 10%

✔ Workload became manageable, and **deadlines were met.**

✔ Startup productivity **doubled** as Amit finally focused on business growth

And Amit? Finally, breathing easily.

💬 "Turns out I didn't need perfect employees—just the right ones with the right plan!"

Key Takeaways for Startup Founders

Problem	Old Situation	New Solution
Unrealistic hiring	Searching for the "perfect" candidate.	Hired for key skills, trained for the rest.
Overcomplicated process	5+ interview rounds.	Streamlined to 2 practical rounds.
High early attrition	No retention plan.	Structured onboarding and career paths.
Founder overwhelmed	Amit is doing everything alone.	Delegation and balanced hiring strategy.

Final Thought: You Don't Need Perfect Employees—Just a Smart Hiring Strategy!

Many startups fail **not** because of bad ideas but because they either **hire too slowly or lose employees quickly.**

By simplifying the hiring process and **building a retention-focused culture**, Amit's startup didn't just survive – it thrived.

So next time you think, *"I just need the right employees to succeed,"* remember: the right employees don't just appear. **You create them with the right approach.**

11

THE REVOLVING DOOR SYNDROME – WHY STAFF KEPT LEAVING THIS BUSINESS

If you ever want to see a business owner lose sleep, look for one whose employees keep quitting. That was Mejo Sebastian, standing in his rice warehouse, staring at another resignation letter. In the past **12 months, he had hired 47 employees**, yet his team never seemed to stay above **8 or 9 people at any given time**.

His FMCG business specialised in **premium rice and rice-based products**. Customers and sales were steady, but what about his workforce? That was a different story. Employees came in, worked for a few months, and disappeared—almost like he was running an unpaid internship for his competitors.

"I hire, I train, and before I even learn their full names, they quit. What am I doing wrong?" Mejo groaned.

He wasn't alone—many businesses in the FMCG sector struggle with employee retention. But instead of accepting high turnover as "normal," we decided to **dig deep and fix the root causes** of this revolving door syndrome.

Step 1: Finding Out Why People Were Quitting

Within a week of speaking to past and current employees, we uncovered **four major issues** pushing people out faster than customers could finish a bag of rice.

1. **The Job Wasn't What They Expected**

   The recruitment ads promised **a dynamic role in a growing FMCG company**. What new hires got was **long hours in a hot warehouse, unpredictable shifts, and endless customer calls**. There was a clear mismatch between expectations and reality.

   🔒 **Problem:** Employees felt misled and left within **3 to 6 months**.

2. **No Career Growth, Just Work**

   The company had roles but no **clear path for promotions or skill development**. Employees were hired to do one thing, and even if they performed well, they remained in the same position.

   🔒 **Problem:** People don't stay in jobs where they see no future.

3. **Leadership Was Absent**

   The managers were focused on **logistics, sales targets and deliveries**, but no one was **managing** the **employees**. There was no mentorship, no structured feedback and no culture of appreciation.

🔒 **Problem:** Employees felt disconnected and unimportant.

4. **No Incentives, Just Salary**

    While competitors were offering **performance-based bonuses, overtime pay, and festival incentives**, Mejo's business relied solely on a **fixed salary**. Hard work was expected but not rewarded.

    🔒 **Problem:** Employees had no financial motivation to stay long-term.

Step 2: Fixing the Revolving Door

1. **Transparent Hiring – No False Promises**

    📌 We rewrote the job descriptions to **accurately reflect the responsibilities and work environment.**

    📌 Every new hire received a **detailed onboarding kit** with role expectations, career growth options and company policies.

    📌 Instead of fancy hiring pitches, we highlighted **stability, learning opportunities, and incentives.**

    ✅ **Result:** New hires **knew what they were signing up for,** reducing **early resignations by 50% in the first six months.**

2. Career Growth – People Stay Where They Grow

📌 Introduced **quarterly training programmes** covering product knowledge, leadership skills, and advanced sales techniques.

📌 Created a **promotion structure**:

+ Warehouse staff could become supervisors in **9-12 months**

+ Sales reps could move into business development in **1-2 years**

+ 📌 Employees who completed training successfully got **salary hikes and title upgrades.**

  ✅ **Result:** Employees **saw a future in the company,** and **internal promotions increased by 45%.**

3. Building a Strong Leadership Culture

📌 Hired an **HR manager** to oversee employee engagement and retention.

📌 Introduced a **buddy system** – each new employee was paired with an experienced team member for mentorship.

📌 Conducted **monthly town hall meetings** where employees could share concerns and suggest improvements.

✅ **Result: Team engagement increased,** and resignation rates **dropped by 40%.**

4. Performance-Based Incentives – Hard Work Pays Off

📌 Sales teams received **commission-based bonuses** for exceeding targets.

📌 Warehouse staff received **incentives for overtime and productivity.**

📌 Festival bonuses and performance-based rewards were introduced for **all employees.**

✅ **Result: Retention improved by 55%,** as employees now had **a financial reason to stay.**

6 Months Later: The Transformation

✔ **Resignation rate dropped by 55%.**

✔ **Average employee tenure increased from 3 months to 1.5 years.**

✔ **Sales team performance improved by 30%.**

✔ **Warehouse efficiency increased by 20%.**

✔ **Employee satisfaction survey showed a 70% improvement.**

And Mejo? No more spending half his time **interviewing and retraining new hires.** His team was finally stable, and his business was scaling without constant disruptions.

💬 **"I was hiring to fill gaps, not to build a team. Now I have 8-9 committed employees at any given time, and we're finally growing the right way."**

Key Takeaways for Business Owners

Problem	Old Situation	New Solution
Hiring Process	Over-promised, under-delivered	Realistic job descriptions and proper onboarding
Career Growth	No training, no promotions	Structured career paths and upskilling programmes
Employee Engagement	No leadership, no guidance	HR intervention and team-building initiatives
Incentives & Motivation	No extra rewards, just workload	Performance-based bonuses and financial perks

Final Thought: Employees Stay Where They Feel Valued

Businesses often focus on **acquiring customers**, but **retaining employees** is just as important. A revolving door of new hires **wastes time, resources and company growth potential**.

By **fixing retention issues**, Mejo created a stable team of 8-9 employees and built a foundation for **scalability, higher profits, and long-term business success.**

12

PERFORMANCE OR POLITICS? – WHEN THE BEST EMPLOYEE WASN'T THE 'BEST'

Gold retail is a high-stakes business. Margins are tight, customer trust is everything, and competition is ruthless. That's why the owner, Anoop Rajan, was baffled when King Royal Jewellers, a prominent gold retailer, faced declining sales despite having a "star performer" in their team.

His **top salesman, Jithin**, had been with the company for five years. He had the best numbers, was the face of the showroom, and Anoop had trusted him blindly. But something felt off.

🔍 **The Problem:** Sales were dropping, employee morale was low, and customer complaints were rising. **Was Jithin really the best employee, or just the best at playing the game?**

Step 1: Investigating the 'Star Performer' Myth

To understand what was happening, we conducted **a detailed assessment of King Royal Jewellers' team performance and work culture.** Here's what we found:

1. **Jithin Was Hoarding Sales**

   While his personal sales numbers were the highest, it turned out that he was **cherry-picking high-value customers** and discouraging other sales staff from handling big-ticket buyers.

   ⚠ **Problem:** Other sales staff were demotivated, leading to **a 30% drop in their performance.**

2. **He Created an 'I'm the Boss' Culture**

   Jithin wasn't just a senior salesperson – he acted like he **owned the showroom.** He would override decisions, manipulate schedules, and undermine the store manager's authority.

   ⚠ **Problem:** Employees hesitated to challenge him, creating **a toxic power structure.**

3. **Customer Service Complaints Had Increased**

   Several **regular customers** mentioned that Jithin prioritised **VIPs and high-value buyers,** making others feel neglected. Some even reported **rushed service and arrogance.**

   ⚠ **Problem:** The brand's reputation was at risk, and **repeat customer visits dropped by 25%.**

4. **He Was Blocking Team Growth**

   Junior employees rarely lasted long because Jithin **controlled training opportunities and**

misled new hires. Some employees even left within six months.

🔒 **Problem:** The company was **losing fresh talent** and relied too much on one person.

Step 2: Fixing the Damage – Strategy for Change

We had a choice: **retrain or replace?** Instead of an immediate removal, we decided to **dismantle Jithin's monopoly and rebuild the sales structure.**

1. **Convincing Jithin to Accept Change**

    We knew confronting Jithin directly would only lead to resistance, so we approached it strategically.

    📌 We **showed him the numbers** – his sales were high, but overall store performance declined. Instead of blaming him, we positioned the discussion around **business growth and sustainability.**

    📌 We gave him a **larger role**—instead of just selling, he was now responsible for **mentoring junior employees** and **guiding high-value customer handling as a team effort.**

    📌 We set clear **performance-linked incentives**—not just for individual sales but also for how well the team performed under his leadership.

    ✅ **Result:** Jithin, though initially hesitant, agreed to the new structure when he saw **a leadership role with financial benefits.**

2. **Restructuring the Sales Model**

📌 Implemented **a fair customer allocation system**—big-ticket clients were now assigned to different team members based on rotation.

📌 Introduced **team-based sales targets** so that incentives weren't just for individuals but for overall store performance.

✅ **Result:** Sales numbers **evened out across the team**, and motivation levels **increased by 40%.**

3. **Restoring Leadership & Authority**

📌 The **store manager's role was reinforced** – all team decisions now had to go through proper channels.

📌 Introduced **weekly performance reviews** where team concerns could be addressed without fear.

✅ **Result:** Employees **felt more secure** and store discipline **improved significantly.**

4. **Customer Experience Overhaul**

📌 Launched a **mystery shopper programme** to evaluate service levels.

📌 Implemented a **customer feedback loop** where all employees were rated on experience, not just sales.

✅ **Result: Customer satisfaction improved by 50%** and repeat buyers **returned to pre-crisis levels.**

5. **Leadership Transition & Team Development**

📌 Trained junior staff on **advanced sales techniques** and customer handling.

📌 Promoted two senior employees to **new leadership roles**, ensuring that no single person dominated the team.

☑ **Result:** New leaders emerged, and **team retention improved by 60%.**

6 Months Later: The Transformation

✔ Sales balanced out across the team.

✔ Employee retention improved from 50% to 80%.

✔ Customer complaints dropped by 70%.

✔ Store revenue increased by 25%.

✔ Jithin adapted to his new role but eventually left. However, the business continued to grow.

Anoop Rajan finally had **a high-performing team – not just one dominant employee.**

💬 "I thought I needed a 'star performer' to drive business. What I really needed was a strong team culture. Now, we're growing the right way."

Key Takeaways for Business Owners

Problem	Old Situation	New Solution
Sales Distribution	One person dominated big sales.	Fair allocation and incentives for all

Problem	Old Situation	New Solution
Workplace Politics	One person controlled decision-making.	Store manager's authority reinforced
Customer Service	VIP bias and rushed service.	Customer feedback and experience focus
Employee Growth	No career progression.	Leadership training and structured promotions

Final Thought: Performance Should Build, Not Break a Team

Sometimes, **your "best employee" is the biggest reason your business isn't growing.** A company should be **bigger than one person**; true performance is about **team success, not individual dominance.**

King Royal Jewellers secured long-term success, stability and customer trust by shifting the focus from one high performer to a well-balanced team.

PART 5

OPERATIONS & SYSTEMISATION STRUGGLES

13

THE BUSINESS THAT RAN ON MEMORY – WHY 'I KNOW EVERYTHING' IS A PROBLEM

It was a scene straight out of the Malayalam movie *Ustad Hotel.* The old hotel bearer, with a towel draped over his shoulder, casually rattled off the day's sales, pending balances, and supplier dues—all from memory. No calculator, no notebook, no system.

Ummer, a character portrayed by the late actor Mamukkoya, was like a human computer: "**86 Porotta, 14 fish curry, 13 chicken curry......**"

The audience chuckled, impressed by his mental maths. But in the real world of business?

That's a **full-blown disaster waiting to happen.**

Scene Shift: A Real Business Running on Thin Air

Meet **Azeem**, owner of **Royal Spices & Rice**, a family-run FMCG business specialising in rice, flour, and spice mixes. His father started the business 40 years ago, and Azeem inherited it with the **most advanced inventory system known to mankind—his brain.**

📌 **Stock levels?** "I know what's in the godown."

📌 **Supplier payments?** "Don't worry, I remember."

📌 **Sales trends?** "No need for software; I've been doing this for years."

And that's exactly why everything started falling apart.

The Disaster Begins

Azeem's **legendary memory** started failing him. Not because he was ageing, but because **his business had grown too big to be run on mental calculations.**

Here's what happened:

📌 **The Great Vanishing Stock Mystery**

One day, a big retail client called.

💬 **"Azeem bhai, where's my order? I paid you for 200 sacks of rice last week!"**

Azeem was sure it was in stock. Except—it wasn't. **Somehow, 50 sacks had "disappeared."**

✴ **Loss:** ₹1.2 Lakhs in missing inventory

📌 Supplier Payments or Magic Tricks?

Azeem prided himself on **never missing payments—** except for the one he did.

💬 **Supplier:** *"Sir, you still haven't paid me for the last flour shipment."*

💬 **Azeem:** *"Of course, I have! You must be mistaken."*

A week later, he found the invoice **crumpled inside his car's glove box.**

✺ **Loss:** Late payment penalties + damaged reputation

📌 The Employee Resignation Chain Reaction

Azeem's staff was **human calculators** trained under his **"Observe and Remember"** method.

💬 **"Sir, we can't keep track of everything as you do."**

💬 **Azeem:** "Just pay attention. You'll learn."

They didn't. **Three senior employees quit** in frustration, leaving Azeem scrambling.

✺ **Loss:** Operational chaos + hiring new (less experienced) staff

📌 The Tax Audit Meltdown

And then, the **ultimate disaster.**

The **tax authorities** showed up.

💬 **Officer:** *"Sir, can we see your purchase records and stock reports?"*

💬 **Azeem:** *"...Umm... I can tell you..."*

Let's just say **they weren't interested in his mental calculations.**

✺ **Loss:** ₹3 Lakhs in fines for **missing documentation**

The Turning Point: "Maybe I Should Write Things Down?"

Azeem **finally admitted defeat.**

💬 *"Fine, tell me what to do."*

We **dragged him—kicking and screaming—into the modern world.**

Step 1: Installing a Simple Inventory System

What We Found:

- Rice stock was **underreported by 20%**
- 10% of deliveries **were made without invoices**
- Frequent **double payments to suppliers**

Solution:

☑ Implemented **the basic digital inventory tool**

☑ Assigned a **storekeeper to record stock movements.**

☑ Introduced **weekly stock audits.**

◆ **Result:** ₹6 Lakhs in **wastage savings within 3 months**

Step 2: Automating Supplier & Payment Records

What We Found:

- ₹2 Lakhs **in forgotten payments**
- ₹1.5 Lakhs **paid twice due to memory-based accounting**

Solution:

☑ Shifted to **accounting software** for purchase tracking.

☑ Introduced a **daily ledger update process.**

☑ Ensured **every transaction was recorded (no exceptions!)**

◈ **Result: Zero missed payments** & **recovered ₹3.5 Lakhs in overpayments**

Step 3: Training Staff to Work Without 'Mental Math'

What We Found:

- Staff **depended on Azeem for every decision**
- No one knew the exact stock levels **without asking him**

Solution:

☑ Created **a role-based access system**—storekeepers, accountants, and sales representatives all had **clear responsibilities.**

☑ Conducted **weekly training** on using systems (not memory).

☑ Introduced **performance incentives** for process adherence.

◈ **Result: Operational efficiency improved by 40%** and **staff morale increased**

Step 4: Preparing for Tax Audits Like a Pro

What We Found:

- **80% of invoices were missing proper documentation**

- Tax reports **were based on "approximate values"**

Solution:

☑ Ensured **all invoices were recorded digitally.**

☑ Introduced **monthly tax compliance reviews**

☑ Partnered with a **professional accountant** for audit preparation.

◈ **Result: Zero fines in the next tax audit** 🎉

6 Months Later: The Transformation

✔ **Inventory mismatches were reduced by 90%.**

✔ **No more supplier payment disputes.**

✔ **Employee satisfaction improved** (no more mental maths anxiety)

✔ **Tax compliance became stress-free.**

Azeem, once **the last defender of the "I Know Everything" business model,** now swears by documentation.

💬 *"I used to think that running a business was about experience and gut feeling. Turns out, systems make you smarter, not weaker."*

Key Takeaways for Business Owners

Problem	Old Situation	New Solution
Stock Tracking	Mental calculation.	Digital inventory system
Supplier Payments	Remembering due dates.	Automated accounting
Employee Dependency	Only the owner knew the details.	Structured Responsibilities
Tax Compliance	Based on estimates.	Proper documentation

Final Thought: Your Brain Is Amazing, But It's Not an ERP System

Running a business **from memory works—until it doesn't.**

A smart entrepreneur **doesn't rely on remembering everything**—they build **systems** so that **nothing needs to be remembered.**

Azeem learned this the hard way. **Do you really want to be the next business to crash because you "had it all in your head"?**

14

PROCESS OR PARALYSIS? – WHEN TOO MANY RULES STOPPED A COMPANY'S GROWTH

Madhu was the kind of businessman who believed in structure. The **founder of Lakshmi Chits**, a well-known chit fund and gold loan company in **South Kerala**, he had built his empire with **discipline, rules and an obsession with documentation.**

His office was a **monument to paperwork**. Rows of steel almirahs groaned under the weight of files dating back to the 1980s. Each transaction, whether a ₹5,000 chit instalment or a ₹10 Lakh gold loan, had at least **six copies of documentation**—signed, sealed, and locked away.

While discipline was his strength, **it was also his downfall.**

The Company That Drowned in Paperwork

Madhu's chit fund business was solid. He ran **over 200 active chit groups**, ranging from ₹50,000 schemes to high-value ₹50 Lakh chits. Additionally, his **gold**

loan portfolio had ₹20 Crores in outstanding loans. The company should have been thriving.

But it wasn't.

While competitors were expanding with **digital KYC, automated disbursals, and online chit auctions**, Lakshmi Chits was stuck in **slow-motion mode.**

Here's what was happening inside:

1. **The Never-Ending Report Syndrome**

   Chit funds require **strict reporting** to track subscriber payments, auction winners, and pending dues. But Madhu had taken it to the extreme.

   📌 **What We Found:**

   ✦ **Daily reports** on subscriber payments

   ✦ **Weekly reports** on auction results

   ✦ **Monthly reports** on pending dues

   ✦ **Quarterly reports** on chit group settlements

   ✦ **Six-monthly reports** comparing performance over the last decade

   Most of these reports **never led to action—** they were just there **because they had always been done.**

   💥 **Result:** Employees spent **60% of their time** making reports instead of actually running the business.

2. Gold Loan Disbursals: A Bureaucratic Nightmare

Gold loans should be **quick**, right? Customers walk in with gold, and they walk out with money.

Not at Lakshmi Chits.

✨ **What We Found:**

✦ Customers had to **fill out four forms** before even getting an evaluation.

✦ The **branch manager needed to approve** every loan manually—even for ₹10,000.

✦ Gold valuation was done by **two separate people,** and if their values differed by even ₹100, the loan was sent for re-evaluation.

💬 **Customer Complaint:** *"I went in for a ₹50,000 gold loan and came out three hours later with nothing. I got the loan in 10 minutes from another company."*

✖ **Result:** Competitors were capturing 70% of new customers while Lakshmi Chits **struggled to retain even existing ones.**

3. The Approval Gridlock

Madhu believed in **signing off on everything himself.**

✦ **Loan settlements?** His approval is needed.

✦ **Chit group auction winner payouts?** Needed his sign-off.

✦ **Even ₹500 petty cash expenses?** Yes, also his signature.

✨ **What We Found:**

- ✦ **200+ files landed on his desk daily**

- ✦ Even the most basic approvals took **3-4 days**

- ✦ Customers left because they had to **wait weeks for simple disbursals**

  ※ **Result:** Competitor chit funds were processing settlements **3 times faster**, making Lakshmi Chits **look outdated and inefficient.**

Fixing the Mess – Without Breaking the System

Madhu knew something wasn't working. **His business wasn't growing, customer retention was falling, and employees were suffocating under excessive rules.**

But change wasn't easy for him.

💬 **Madhu:** *"We can't just remove processes! That's what keeps us disciplined."*

We had to **show him the numbers—exactly how much business he was losing due to his rigid system.**

◈ Step 1: Automating Reports & Cutting the Junk

What We Found:

- **30% of reports were unnecessary**

- Staff spent **4-5 hours daily** preparing them

✅ Solution:

- Eliminated **daily manual reporting** (moved to an auto-generated dashboard)

- Kept **only 3 key reports**: Weekly Subscriber Status, Auction Summary, and Loan Performance

- Set up **real-time alerts** for overdue payments instead of printed reports

◈ Result:

- **40% reduction in admin workload**

- Staff had more time to **focus on customers** instead of spreadsheets

◈ Step 2: Fixing the Gold Loan Approval Madness

What We Found:

- Average loan processing time was **3 hours**

- **50% of customers** left due to delays

☑ Solution:

- Loans under ₹1 Lakh **approved instantly** by branch managers

- Introduced **digital valuation** with standardised pricing

- **Mobile OTP approvals** for repeat customers instead of re-verification

◈ Result:

- **Loan processing time reduced from 3 hours to 15 minutes**

- **Customer retention improved by 25%** in 6 months

◈ Step 3: Delegating Approvals

What We Found:

- Madhu was handling 200+ approvals daily

- 90% of these were small-ticket transactions

☑ Solution:

- Set limits:

    ✦ ₹50,000 & below → Branch Manager approval

    ✦ ₹50,000 – ₹5 Lakhs → Regional Manager approval

    ✦ Above ₹5 Lakhs → Madhu's approval

◈ Result:

- Processing time dropped by 70%

- Madhu could focus on **strategy instead of signatures**

6 Months Later: The Transformation

✔ Customer complaints dropped by 60%

✔ Gold loan disbursals increased by 45%.

✔ Employee efficiency improved by 35%.

✔ New chit group enrollments grew by 25%.

Madhu, the man who once believed in **rules over results,** now saw the value of **process efficiency.**

💬 **Madhu:** *"We still have discipline. The only difference is— now our rules work for us, not against us."*

Key Takeaways for Business Owners

Problem	Old System	New System
Too Many Reports	Manual reports are eating up time.	Automated dashboards
Gold Loan Delays	Multiple approvals, slow process.	Instant loans under ₹1 lakh
Approval Bottlenecks	Madhu signing everything.	Delegated authority to managers

Final Thought: Are You Stuck in 'Process Paralysis'?

A business **without rules is chaos.**

But a business **drowning in rules is just as bad.**

Madhu learned that **efficiency doesn't mean compromising discipline – it means making discipline work smarter.**

The question is—**Is your business running on processes, or is it stuck in them?**

15

THE ONE-MAN SHOW TRAP – THE FOUNDER WHO COULDN'T LET GO

Jazeer was **not just the founder** of Dew Springs, a premium **mineral water brand** in the **High Ranges of Kerala.** He was its **CEO, marketing head, operations manager, sales supervisor, quality inspector, HR executive, and sometimes even its truck driver.**

To say he was hands-on would be an understatement.

If a **new distributor was onboarded**, Jazeer was there, shaking hands and explaining the product.

If a **machine needed maintenance**, he was there, sleeves rolled up, inspecting every nut and bolt.

If a **customer complained**, Jazeer personally called to apologise—even if it was just about a missing label.

And at the end of the day, when the last truck left the bottling plant, he'd sit at his desk, exhausted, staring at the **hundreds of pending tasks only he could handle.**

That's when the calls would start.

"**Sir, the bank needs your signature for the new account.**"

"**Jazeer bhai, we need approval for next month's ad campaign.**"

"**Sir, our distributor in Ernakulam is threatening to leave. Can you talk to him?**"

Jazeer sighed. The **company had grown**, but somehow, **he was busier than ever.**

Dew Springs: A Brand Held Together by One-Man

It wasn't that Dew Springs was struggling. The business had done well:

✦ **Annual turnover: ₹18 Crores**

✦ **Production capacity: 50,000 litres/day**

✦ **Presence in 10 districts of Kerala**

✦ **120+ distributors and over 3,000 retail outlets**

But growth had **stalled.**

Jazeer was stretched **too thin**. Every decision required his approval, and every problem landed on his desk. Employees had stopped taking initiative because they knew, at the end of the day, "**Sir will handle it.**"

And he did. Until he couldn't.

🔖 The Breaking Point

One day, a **major supermarket chain** approached Dew Springs.

💬 **"We want to stock your brand across our 50 outlets."**

It was a **huge opportunity** – a chance to scale across **Kerala's premium retail sector.**

But there was one problem.

To meet the **demand**, Dew Springs **needed to double production.** That meant:

✅ **Hiring new staff**

✅ **Upgrading the bottling plant**

✅ **Expanding logistics**

And guess who had to **handle everything?**

Jazeer.

He tried for two months. He negotiated with suppliers, interviewed factory workers, reviewed machine upgrades, **and personally inspected new warehouse spaces.**

Meanwhile, his existing **business started crumbling.**

✦ **Delivery delays increased by 40%**

✦ **Five key distributors left** due to poor communication

✦ **His best plant supervisor resigned**, saying: *"Sir, we can't keep waiting for approvals that never come."*

✖ **Result:** He had to **drop the supermarket deal** because **he simply didn't have the bandwidth to handle it.**

That's when he realised—his company wasn't **scaling** because **he wasn't letting it.**

🔍 Our Diagnosis: The One-Man Show Trap

When we stepped in, it was clear that Jazeer wasn't running a business; **he was running himself into the ground.**

Here's what we found:

1. **No Delegation, Only 'Jazeer Approval'**

   Everything—**from marketing to minor expense approvals—required his sign-off.**

   📌 **Example:** Even a ₹3,000 ad spend on social media needed his **personal review.**

   ❋ Impact: Employees **stopped making decisions** and work piled up on Jazeer's desk.

2. **Zero Middle Management**

   The company had **over 100 employees**, but no proper **managers.**

   📌 **Example:**

   ✦ **The sales team reported directly to him.**

   ✦ **Factory workers waited for his nod on even routine maintenance.**

   ✦ **Distributors escalated every issue straight to Jazeer.**

      ❋ Impact: Jazeer became a **bottleneck** instead of a leader.

3. **Lack of Systems & Processes**

   There were **no SOPs (Standard Operating Procedures)** in place.

📌 **Example:**

✦ **Distributor onboarding?** No process, just a handshake deal.

✦ **Customer complaints?** No tracking system, only WhatsApp messages.

✦ **Employee roles?** Everyone did **everything**— but nothing got done.

✴ **Impact:** The company relied on **memory and habit** instead of structured processes.

🛠 The Fix: Turning a One-Man Show into a Scalable Business

To **free** Jazeer from his own trap, we took three major steps:

🔷 Step 1: Creating a Middle Management Layer

☑ **Hired a GM (General Manager)** to take over **daily operations.**

☑ Promoted two senior staff members to **Sales & Operations Heads.**

☑ Gave them **decision-making authority** for all **routine approvals.**

🔷 Result:

- **75% of operational work moved off Jazeer's plate**

- Faster decision-making without waiting for **"Sir's approval"**

◈ Step 2: Implementing a Delegation Framework

☑ Introduced a 'Decision Matrix'

- ✦ **₹10,000 & below:** The team can approve

- ✦ **₹10,000 – ₹1 Lakh:** GM approves

- ✦ **Above ₹1 Lakh:** Needs Jazeer's review

  ☑ **Sales, HR and Logistics now had clear responsibilities.**

  ☑ **Weekly meetings replaced constant phone calls**

◈ Result:

- **Distributor complaints dropped by 60%**

- Jazeer had time to **focus on growth, not daily firefighting**

◈ Step 3: Systematising the Business

☑ **Set up CRM software** for distributor tracking.

☑ **Created SOPs for every key process** (onboarding, order processing, payments).

☑ **Customer complaints are now logged and resolved within 24 hours**

◈ Result:

- Faster **order processing** = happier distributors

- More **organised operations** = less chaos

6 Months Later: The Transformation

✔ **Supermarket deal back on track**

✔ **Sales increased by 30%** due to better distributor management.

✔ **Customer complaint resolution time reduced by 50%.**

✔ **Jazeer finally took his first vacation in 5 years!**

💬 **Jazeer:** *"I thought I was the only one who could run this business. Turns out, I was the only one stopping it from running better."*

Key Takeaways for Entrepreneurs

Problem	Old System	New System
Everything depended on Jazeer.	No delegation.	Middle managers in place
No decision-making authority for employees.	All approvals needed his nod.	Structured approval system
Business had no defined processes.	Ran on memory and habit.	SOPs for every major task

Final Thought: Are You the Growth Blocker in Your Own Business?

Every entrepreneur starts as a **one-man army.** But if your business **can't function without you,** then you don't own a business—you own a full-time job.

Jazeer learned that **letting go doesn't mean losing control**—it means gaining the freedom to grow.

The question is—**Are you ready to step back so your business can step forward?**

PART 6

MARKETING & SALES PITFALLS

16

THE SALES TEAM THAT NEVER SOLD – A MASTERCLASS IN WASTING TIME

How 10 Salespeople Spent Their Days Talking, Drinking Coffee, and Achieving Absolutely Nothing!

Meet "Strategic" Sanoj – The CEO Who Thought Sales Was a 'Mindset'

Sanoj was the **founder of a premium office furniture company** called **LuxWork Interiors.**

The business had everything going for it:

☑ **High-end chairs and desks** that made CEOs feel like kings.

☑ A **fancy showroom** with glass walls and mood lighting.

☑ A **sales team of 10 people**—who, shockingly, **never sold anything.**

Yep.

Despite **having 10 full-time salespeople**, sales were as rare as a **Wi-Fi connection in the Himalayas.**

Sanoj was **confused and frustrated.**

✦ "I don't get it! My team is always busy!"

✦ "They go to meetings, attend seminars, do follow-ups... but where are the orders?"

✦ "Are my salespeople actually... just meeting people for fun?"

I didn't have the heart to answer that last question.

The Discovery: When Salesmen Become 'Meeting Consultants'

I decided to **follow the sales team** for a week.

What I found **shocked me to my core.**

1. **Meeting Mania – Because Talking Feels Productive!**

   ◆ The team **loved meetings.** They scheduled them **for everything.**

   ◆ Every meeting was **at least 2 hours long,** full of **"strategic discussions."**

   ◆ The problem? **No one ever asked for the order!**

   A typical conversation went like this:

   Salesperson: *"Sir, our ergonomic chairs will increase your productivity!"*

   Client: *"Sounds great. What's the price?"*

Salesperson: *"Sir, let's schedule another meeting to discuss that."*

Another meeting? For what?

These guys treated meetings **like Netflix episodes** – they just kept making more without ever finishing the story.

2. **The Follow-Up Loop of Doom**

If a potential customer **did not respond**, the team had one brilliant strategy:

📞 **Call them again.**

✉ **Email them again.**

📝 **Send another "Just checking in" message.**

If the client ignores them 10 times? No problem!

They would **follow-up 20 more times**—but still **never close the deal.**

It was like watching **a guy keep texting his ex, hoping for a miracle.**

3. **The "Research" Scam**

Sanoj's team had another **ingenious excuse** for low sales:

👉 **"We are doing research."**

What research?!

+ They spent **days making competitor reports.**

+ They **analysed market trends** instead of selling.

✦ They created **PowerPoint presentations** instead of making calls.

One salesman even told me, "**I am working on a 32-slide deck about the future of office chairs.**"

I stared at him.

"**But have you sold even one office chair?**"

He smiled nervously. "**Not yet, but the research is amazing.**"

The Fix: How We Turned "Meeting Experts" Into Actual Salespeople

Step 1: The 'One Meeting' Rule 🚀

We implemented **the golden rule:**

⬤ **One meeting per client.**

◑ **No endless follow-ups.**

◑ **Ask for the sale immediately.**

No more coffee-drinking strategy sessions.

If a client wants another meeting, they must first confirm the order.

Sales instantly **jumped by 40%.**

Step 2: The "Follow-Up Only Twice" Rule

We banned **the never-ending follow-up cycle.**

✅ **First follow-up:** A simple reminder.

✅ **Second follow-up:** *"Are you interested? If not, we'll move on."*

If the client **ignored both**, we **moved on** to new leads.

(Salesmen **cried**, but I assured them they'd live.)

Step 3: The "Stop Overthinking" Method

We **banned useless research.**

📌 **No more 50-slide presentations.**

📌 **No more competitor analysis every week.**

📌 **JUST SELL!**

If a customer wanted data, we sent them **a simple one-page brochure.**

Nothing more.

Sales doubled in three months.

The Transformation – From Talkers to Closers

✅ **Meetings reduced by 70%.**

✅ **The average deal closure time dropped from 4 months to 3 weeks.**

✅ **Sanoj's company finally started making money.**

✅ **Salespeople finally understood that their job is to SELL—not to "explore synergies."**

The best part?

Sanoj no longer had to **beg his sales team to work.**

Now, they were **excited** because they were **earning commissions like never before!**

Lessons for Entrepreneurs: How to Fix a Sales Team That Doesn't Sell

Problem	Why It's Bad	Solution
Too many meetings	Wastes time, no progress.	Limit to **one meeting per client.**
Endless follow-ups	Clients get annoyed.	**Follow-up only twice**
Too much research	Avoids real work.	**Sell, don't overthink**
No closing strategy	Clients never commit.	**Always ask for the sale.**
Salespeople are afraid to ask	No deals get done.	**Make asking for orders a habit.**

Final Thoughts: Your Sales Team Is Not a Consulting Firm!

Sanoj's mistake?

He let his sales team **act like business analysts instead of salespeople.**

The business finally took off once we encouraged them to focus on closing deals instead of having endless meetings.

And the best part?

For the first time, Sanoj **stopped worrying about money**—because sales were happening!

17

BRANDING CHAOS – HOW ONE BUSINESS CONFUSED ITS OWN CUSTOMERS

When we first met Anees, the owner of SparkleCare Cleaning Solutions, he was pacing around his office, visibly frustrated.

"We have the best cleaning liquid in the market," he declared, slamming a competitor's bottle on the table. "But sales aren't growing. Customers love the product, but somehow, they're not sticking to our brand."

We had heard this story before. We didn't expect the level of branding confusion we were about to uncover.

🧴 The Great Cleaning Liquid Identity Crisis

Anees's company specialises in one thing: cleaning liquids. But here's where things got messy.

Instead of building one strong brand, he launched four different brands—all selling the same type of cleaning liquid.

That's right. Four brands. One product category.

Each had its name, logo, colour scheme, and even a different marketing angle.

Brand 1: SparkleX – Marketed as a "power cleaner" for professionals.

◉ Sold in hardware stores

◉ Bold, industrial-looking packaging

◉ Advertised as "For the Toughest Stains"

Brand 2: PureFresh – Positioned as an eco-friendly cleaner.

◉ Sold in organic & health stores

◉ Pastel-coloured bottle with a leaf symbol

◉ Slogan: "Nature's Clean Touch"

Brand 3: HomeShine – Marketed for families.

◉ Sold in supermarkets.

◉ Bright yellow bottle with a smiling cartoon bubble

◉ Slogan: "Safe for Your Home, Tough on Dirt"

Brand 4: GermoKill – Pushed as an antibacterial cleaner.

◉ Sold in pharmacies & online

◉ Clinical white packaging with "99.9% Germ Kill" in bold

◉ Slogan: "Healthier Homes, Safer Lives"

🔧 Result? Absolute confusion.

Customers had no idea that all four brands came from the same company – and worse, they often competed against each other on store shelves.

Retailers were equally frustrated. Some stocked only one or two brands, thinking the others were from competitors.

Sales weren't adding up. Instead of consolidating a loyal customer base, SparkleCare split its market share across four identities.

📊 The Brand Audit: What We Found

After a few weeks of market research, retailer interviews, and customer surveys, we presented our findings to Anees:

☑ Customers were confused. Many who loved HomeShine had never even heard of SparkleX.

☑ Retailers didn't know the products were from the same company. Some even placed them side by side, making them compete.

☑ Marketing costs were out of control. Running separate campaigns for four different brands meant quadruple the ad spend with no added brand strength.

☑ Loyalty was impossible to build. Customers couldn't stick to one brand because they didn't realise they already used the same company's product under a different name!

Anees finally saw the problem. "We're not building a brand – we're running four small, weak brands against each other."

🛠 The 1-Year Branding Transformation

We designed a step-by-step rebranding strategy to bring clarity to the business without losing existing customers.

◈ Month 1-3: Merging the Brands

☑ After analysing sales data, we retired three brands and consolidated everything under one master brand: SparkleCare.

☑ Redesigned a strong brand identity—a unified logo, colour scheme, and packaging.

☑ Reworked the slogan to: "Powerful. Safe. Trusted."

💡 Result: A clear identity. Customers now recognise the product instantly instead of mistaking it for different brands.

◈ Month 4-6: Educating the Market

☑ Launched a marketing campaign to announce the rebranding:

- ✦ "Same trusted quality, now under ONE name!"
- ✦ Showed the transition from four brands to one.

☑ Ran retailer workshops to explain the changes.

☑ Trained the sales team to guide customers through the transition.

💡 Result: Instead of losing customers, sales actually increased by 18% as brand trust improved.

◈ Month 7-9: Strengthening Market Presence

☑ Launched combo packs in supermarkets to introduce existing customers to the new brand identity.

☑ Standardised pricing and offers, avoiding competing price points among previous brands.

💡 Result: Retailers ordered 30% more stock as they no longer had to manage multiple brands with different margins.

◈ Month 10-12: Expanding with a Stronger Brand

☑ Leveraged the new brand recognition to enter 100 more supermarkets and 50 hardware stores.

☑ Streamlined advertising costs—previously split between four brands—saving 35% on marketing while doubling the impact.

💡 Final Result:

☑ Sales increased by 40% in one year.

📣 Marketing efficiency doubled.

💰 Retailers expanded shelf space for

◎ Key Takeaways for Business Owners

Problem	Before Consulting	After 1-year strategy
Too many brands	4 competing brands in one category	1 strong master brand

Problem	Before Consulting	After 1-year strategy
Marketing inefficiency	High costs, scattered ads	Single, focused campaign
Customer confusion.	Customers are unaware of the brand connection.	Clear brand identity.
Retailer frustration	Stocking multiple "competing" products	Easy, standardised stocking

💡 The Final Lesson: Don't Fight Yourself in the Market

Anees had the right product all along. The only thing standing in the way was his own branding strategy.

The moral of the story?

🔖 Your brand should compete with competitors, not with itself.

One strong brand beats four weak, confusing ones.

At the end of our one year consulting assignment, Anees shook hands with us, smiling.

"Thank God we cleaned up our own mess," he joked.

18

Digital Marketing Disaster – The Business That Burnt Lakhs on Ads With No ROI

When we first met **Rekha**, the founder of **The White Elephant**, she was staring at her laptop screen as if it had personally betrayed her.

"I don't get it," she sighed, rubbing her temples. "I've spent over ₹15 **lakhs** on Instagram and Facebook ads in the last year… and I still have **zero profit to show for it.**"

We leaned in. "Okay. Let's start with the basics. How many sales have you actually made from these ads?"

Rekha blinked. "I… don't really know."

That's when we knew this was going to be **a long conversation.**

🛍️ The Boutique That Loved the 'Boost' Button

Rekha's boutique, **The White Elephant**, specialises in **handcrafted designer wear**—sarees, salwars, and

Indo-Western outfits with intricate embroidery. The products were stunning, and the craftsmanship was impeccable.

But the digital marketing? **A total disaster.**

Like many small business owners, Rekha believed a little too much in the "Boost Post" button on Instagram and Facebook.

Every time she posted a new outfit, she **invested ₹20,000–₹50,000** in boosting it—without a strategy, target audience research, or even checking if it converted to sales.

🛍️ Result?

- Tonnes of **likes, comments, and shares…** but no actual purchases.

- Followers increasing, but **they were mostly window shoppers or bots.**

- A draining ad budget with **no return on investment.**

Rekha wasn't running **ads**—she was just **donating money to Meta.**

📊 What We Found (The Painful Truth)

After a deep dive into her ad manager and sales data, here's what we uncovered:

✅ She was targeting the wrong audience.

- ◆ Ads were **reaching 18-year-old students** who loved her designs but couldn't afford a ₹7,000 saree.

- ✦ Instead of attracting real buyers, she got **engagement from people without intention of purchasing.**

✅ **Her website had significant friction points.**

- ✦ No proper checkout process.

- ✦ Payment gateway glitches.

- ✦ No WhatsApp integration for easy order placement.

- ✦ Many interested buyers **dropped off without completing their purchase.**

✅ **There was no retargeting strategy.**

- ✦ People browsed the website but never got reminders to return.

- ✦ No follow-up emails, no WhatsApp nudges—nothing.

✅ **She was competing with herself.**

- ✦ She posted **too many different types of products.**

- ✦ Instead of building one strong identity, she was **all over the place**—traditional sarees one day, trendy fusion wear the next, casual kurtis the day after.

- ✦ Customers didn't understand what **The White Elephant stood for.**

🕵 Rekha's reaction?

She stared at us wide-eyed. "So basically... I paid Instagram to confuse my customers?"

Pretty much.

📌 The 6-Month Turnaround Strategy

We needed **a complete digital marketing reset.**

◈ Month 1-2: Fixing the Basics

☑ **Defined her ideal customer** – Working women aged 28–45, urban, interested in premium ethnic wear.

☑ **Cleaned up the website** – Faster checkout, WhatsApp ordering, and proper product categories.

☑ **Started retargeting ads** – So people who visited once saw reminders & offers.

💡 **Result:** Engagement dropped (because bots don't buy clothes), but **real inquiries increased.**

◈ Month 3-4: Smart Ad Strategy, Not Just Boosting

☑ **Launched lead generation ads** – We collected customer information for follow-ups instead of just showing products.

☑ **Used dynamic retargeting** – So if someone viewed a saree, they got ads specifically for sarees, not random dresses.

☑ **Stopped targeting broke students** – Ads were adjusted for income level & shopping behaviour.

💡 **Result:** 32% increase in direct messages asking for product details.

◈ Month 5-6: Building Brand Loyalty

✅ **Ran WhatsApp drip campaigns** – Sending styling tips, discount offers, and festive collections to previous buyers.

✅ **Encouraged influencer marketing** – Instead of throwing money at ads, we sent outfits to **real fashion influencers** to showcase in everyday settings.

✅ **Created a limited-edition festive collection** – Generating urgency & exclusivity.

💡 Result:

☑ Sales jumped **by 48% in six months.**

💰 Ad spend reduced **by 40%, but ROI improved.**

🎯 More targeted traffic—**no more wasted clicks from random teenagers**

📣 Final Takeaway: It's Not About Spending More, It's About Spending Smart

Mistake	Before Consulting	After Strategy
Ad Targeting	Random people, no filtering	Defined buyer persona
Budget Usage	₹15 million wasted on boosting	₹8L spent with **ROI-focused ads**
Website Conversions	Low, confusing checkout.	Seamless, easy-to-buy process

Mistake	Before Consulting	After Strategy
Customer Follow-Up	None	Retargeting and WhatsApp drip campaigns

At the end of six months, Rekha wasn't just relieved—she was **shocked.**

"I actually **spent less** than before," she said. "And I finally have **real customers, not just random likes.**"

Lesson?

🔖 **Boosting posts isn't digital marketing. It's digital gambling.**

If you don't have a strategy, **you're just burning money.**

And trust us—**Instagram doesn't feel bad when you do.**

PART 7

LEADERSHIP & GROWTH CHALLENGES

19

EXPANSION GONE WRONG – THE BUSINESS THAT OPENED A NEW BRANCH AND LOST BOTH

When **Faizal**, the owner of **Elite Tiles & Bathware**, decided to expand his business, he was convinced it was the best decision of his career.

For years, his showroom in **South Kerala** has been a leader in the industry, generating around ₹2 crores in monthly revenue from a steady stream of contractors, architects, and retail customers.

But then came the **big idea**—why not open a second branch in another city? It was a growing market, and demand for premium sanitary ware increased.

"I thought it was a no-brainer," Faizal admitted later. "More locations, more sales, more profit—right?"

Wrong. **Six months after opening the new branch, both locations were struggling, and he was burning through cash just to keep the business afloat.**

🛁 The 'Bigger is Better' Trap

Faizal's logic wasn't completely flawed. **Expansion is a natural step for any growing business.** But there's a big difference between a **well-planned expansion** and a **disaster waiting to happen.**

Here's where things started falling apart:

1. **The New Branch Became a Cash Black Hole**

   ♦ Setting up the new showroom required an upfront investment of ₹**3.5 crores** (₹2 crore for interiors, ₹1 crore for initial stock, and ₹50 lakhs for branding & launch).

   ♦ Monthly rent? ₹**6 lakhs.**

   ♦ Staff salaries? ₹**4.5 lakhs per month** for a team of 15 employees.

   ♦ Marketing & promotions? ₹**2 lakhs per month.**

   🔔 **Total monthly expenses for the new branch: ₹12.5–₹13 lakhs.**

   But **the revenue never took off.** In the first three months, the new showroom barely touched ₹**40 lakhs per month**—not even enough to cover operating costs, let alone generate profit.

2. **The Existing Showroom Started Suffering**

   Inventory issues: Faizal couldn't maintain a fresh stock at his original showroom since a lot of cash was tied up in the new branch. Popular models were out of stock for weeks.

Staff stretched too thin: His senior sales team, experts at closing big deals, were now managing two locations, leading to a **dip in customer service quality.**

Marketing efforts got diluted: Instead of focusing on a **strong, single market**, resources were being spread across two locations—resulting in **weaker branding and reduced footfall.**

🔒 **The result:** Sales in the original showroom **dropped from ₹2 crores to ₹1.6 crores per month in just four months.**

3. **Pricing & Credit Policy Made It Worse**

♦ To **attract new customers**, Faizal offered heavy discounts at the new branch. But this **ate into margins** and confused existing customers.

♦ Some **big contractors demanded the same lower prices** at the first showroom. **Loyal customers felt cheated.**

♦ To manage cash flow, Faizal **started extending more credit** to wholesale buyers. Within months, his **outstanding payments crossed ₹3.5 crores**—and collecting dues became a nightmare.

🔒 **By month six, he was stuck in a loop—more sales but less money in hand.**

📊 What We Found (And How We Fixed It)

When we stepped in, Faizal was **already in panic mode.** He was juggling supplier debts, employee complaints, and the fear of **shutting down one of the branches.**

✅ Step 1: Fixing the Inventory & Cash Flow

📌 **Stopped overstocking:**

- Instead of investing money in a **huge upfront inventory,** we **shifted to a 'just-in-time' model**—only stocking fast-moving products and **ordering the rest based on demand.**

- This freed up **₹1.2 crores in working capital.**

📌 **Revised credit policy:**

- Limited credit sales to **trusted contractors.**

- Introduced a **5% cash discount** for early payments.

- Within 3 months, the outstanding dues **dropped from ₹3.5 crores to ₹2 crores.**

✅ Step 2: Making the New Branch Profitable

📌 **Increased product visibility:**

- We **redesigned the showroom layout** to make premium collections stand out.

- Used **WhatsApp marketing** to send daily product updates to contractors and architects.

📌 **Stopped price-cutting madness:**

- ✦ Instead of **random discounts**, we created **bundled offers**—for example, Buy premium tiles and get bathroom fittings at 20% off.

- ✦ This **increased average billing size from ₹50,000 to ₹85,000 per customer.**

📌 **Targeted the right customers:**

- ✦ Instead of generic ads, we **ran hyperlocal campaigns targeting new home builders.**

- ✦ Within 4 months, the new showroom's revenue **jumped from ₹40L to ₹80L per month.**

✅ Step 3: Bringing the Original Showroom Back to Strength

📌 **Refocused marketing:**

- ✦ Stopped **splitting advertising budgets** and positioned the first showroom as the **premium experience centre**, making the second showroom an **affordable home solutions hub.**

- ✦ This **cleared the brand confusion** and brought back high-value customers.

📌 **Incentivised sales team:**

- ✦ Introduced **commission-based incentives** for cross-selling high-margin products.

- ✦ Within **2 months, sales staff performance improved, and the first showroom's revenue was back to ₹1.9 crores per month.**

🏆 The One Year Turnaround

Problem	Before Consulting	After Strategy
New Showroom Monthly Sales	₹40L	₹80L
Original Showroom Monthly Sales	₹1.6Cr (dropped from ₹2Cr)	₹1.9Cr (recovering)
Inventory Investment	₹3.5Cr (upfront)	₹1.2Cr (freed up with demand-based stocking)
Outstanding Credit Dues	₹3.5Cr	₹2Cr
Monthly Business Loss	₹13L	₹5L profit from both locations

By **month 12**, Faizal's showrooms were no longer in survival mode. Instead of shutting one down, both locations were **functioning profitably – with clear positioning, controlled costs, and sustainable growth.**

📣 The Lesson: Growth is Good, But Only If It's Smart!

Expanding a business **should never be an emotional decision.** More locations don't always mean **more profits.** If not planned properly, **you might lose your existing business while chasing a new one.**

Before opening a new branch, **ask these questions:**

✅ Do I have the financial buffer to sustain losses for at least 6 months?

✅ Can I maintain product quality, pricing and customer experience in both locations?

✅ Is my supply chain ready to handle multiple outlets?

Faizal learned it the hard way. But thanks to the structured approach, he **turned things around—** without losing either branch.

And the next time he plans an expansion? **You can bet he's calling us first.**

20

THE PARTNERSHIP PROBLEM – FRIENDS IN BUSINESS, ENEMIES IN LIFE

Moosa and Kareem had been inseparable since childhood. They went to the same school, played on the same football team, and even got into trouble together. Naturally, when they hit their 40s and decided to **start a furniture manufacturing business**, it seemed like a match made in heaven.

After all, they had **one thing in common** – a deep love for premium furniture.

Moosa had **worked in marketing for 15 years** and believed in **branding and customer experience.**

Kareem was a **factory operations expert** who knew the ins and outs of production.

With ₹12 **crores** pooled from their savings, bank loans, and a few investors, they launched **Wood Royale**, a **high-end furniture manufacturing brand** with plans to dominate the South Kerala market.

Their vision? **A showroom that looked like a luxury home and a factory that could produce 500 premium units a month.**

Their reality? **Within two years, they were drowning in ₹6 crores of debt and weren't even on talking terms.**

🚗 The Grand (and Expensive) Launch

Moosa and Kareem didn't start small. Oh no. They went **big**.

Here's what they set up:

🏭 **A 25,000 sq ft factory** in a prime industrial area – ₹4.5 crores investment

🏬 **A showroom in a high-end locality** – ₹1.8 crores for interiors and branding

🔧 **Imported Italian machinery** – ₹2.5 crores upfront payment

👷 **A team of 40 workers and 6 sales staff** – ₹18 lakhs per month in salaries

📢 **Marketing budget for social media, influencers, and newspaper ads** – ₹70 lakhs/year

They expected to recover all of this within **three years.**

By month 6, **they were already in trouble.**

📋 The Three Biggest Mistakes That Killed the Business

1. **The Showroom vs. Factory War**

Moosa believed that **branding was king**.

- He insisted on a showroom that looked like a **luxury villa.**

- ₹22 lakhs was spent on **custom lighting and display units** alone.

- He pushed for **celebrity endorsements**, roping in an actor for a ₹40 lakh campaign.

Kareem, on the other hand, **was all about the numbers.**

- He wanted to focus on **wholesale orders to interior designers and builders.**

- He argued that the showroom was **"a ₹1.8 crore waste"** and preferred direct sales.

🔒 **Fight #1:** Kareem discovered Moosa had spent another **₹15 lakhs on PR events** without informing him.

Moosa's logic: "We need visibility to attract premium clients!"

Kareem's logic: "We need to survive first!"

Both were right, but **the business was bleeding money.**

2. **The Inventory and Cash Flow Disaster**

Moosa's 'luxury' vision meant every furniture piece was **made-to-order**, using the finest materials.

- **Production time?** 45-60 days.

- **Raw materials?** ₹1.2 crores worth of high-end wood sitting in the warehouse.

- **Orders in hand?** Only **40-50 units per month**, nowhere near the **300 needed to break even.**

Kareem started producing **cheaper, ready-made furniture** for quick sales.

- This **confused customers**—was Wood Royale a high-end custom brand or a mass market supplier?

- **Result?** Neither segment trusted them fully.

🔒 **Fight #2:** When Moosa learned that Kareem **had secretly taken bulk orders** from a mid-range retailer, he flipped.

- **Moosa's argument:** "We are a premium brand, not a wholesale factory!"

- **Kareem's response:** "And what will we do with all this wood? Burn it?"

3. **The Salary and Vendor Crisis**

- **By Month 8**, suppliers started **demanding advance payments** because ₹95 **lakhs in pending bills** had piled up.

- **By Month 10, workers' salaries were delayed twice.**

- **By Month 12, the factory accountant quit, saying, 'I don't do divorce cases.'**

  🔒 **Fight #3:** Kareem accused Moosa of **"burning money on nonsense,"** while Moosa accused Kareem of **"making us look like a roadside furniture shop."**

It escalated so much that **they stopped speaking to each other**, and workers had to get approvals from **both partners separately**, causing **massive delays**.

◹ The Final Collapse

- **Month 1:** Sales hit ₹80 lakhs, and everything looked promising.

- **Month 6:** Sales slowed to ₹55 lakhs, but expenses remained at ₹1.2 crores/month.

- **Month 12:** ₹3 crores of losses, tensions running high.

- **Month 18:** ₹6 crores in debt, showroom running at **one-fourth capacity**.

By year 2, **it was over**.

Kareem walked away, **selling his stake for just ₹80 lakhs** (a fraction of his investment).

Moosa tried to **reposition the brand**, but with the debt load, it was impossible.

Wood Royale shut down in less than three years.

🔎 **The Post-Mortem: Why It Failed**

📌 **No Clear Leadership Roles:** Moosa and Kareem never defined **who was in charge of what.**

📌 **Conflicting Business Models:** Was it luxury? Was it a mass market? Even their customers were confused.

📌 **Cash Flow Mismanagement:** They spent big without ensuring a **consistent revenue stream.**

📌 **Ego Battles:** Instead of solving problems, **they fought over who was "right".**

🎭 The Lesson? Business Partnerships Are Like Marriages

🔐 **Just because you're best friends doesn't mean you'll be good business partners.**

Moosa and Kareem failed **not because they weren't smart** but because they **didn't align their vision and execution.**

If you're thinking about starting a business with a friend, ask yourself:

✅ Do we have **clearly defined roles?**

✅ Do we agree on the **business model and target** market?

✅ Can we **keep emotions out of decision-making?**

Because if you don't, **you might lose your money and your best friend.**

21

SCALING SMARTLY – THE STORY OF A BUSINESS THAT FINALLY GOT IT RIGHT

Shakeer and Shinas were the classic **"Let's do something big"** duo. Childhood friends from Kerala had spent years talking about starting a business. Every chai break turned into a brainstorming session. One day, they decided to **stop talking and start pouring.**

That's how **"Chai Junction"** was born – a small, cosy tea shop with a modern twist.

Within **three years, they expanded to 30+ outlets,** built a scalable system, and created a cult following. Unlike many businesses that **crashed under rapid expansion**, Chai Junction **scaled the smart way**—and we had the privilege of guiding them from day one.

🍵 The Beginning: A Tea Shop With a Difference

Their first outlet was a **tiny 200 sq ft shop near a college**, set up with just ₹7 **lakhs in savings**. But instead of being just another *chai kada,* Shakeer and Shinas did things differently:

☑ **Branding:** They created a **trendy, Instagrammable space** with a retro aesthetic.

☑ **Signature Menu:** They didn't just serve chai; they had **"flavoured chai shots,"** *kulhad chai,* **and seasonal specials.**

☑ **Pricing Strategy:** A cup of tea started at ₹15, but the premium blends increased to ₹80.

☑ **Customer Experience:** Every chai was **served with a smile** and a **quick chat**—a simple but powerful retention tool.

Within **six months**, they were making **₹5 lakhs per month** from that single outlet.

That's when they came to us and said, **"We want to open 10 more outlets."**

🚀 The Common Expansion Mistake (That They Didn't Make)

Most small business owners, when they see success, **blindly open more outlets** without thinking about:

✗ **Cashflow Planning**

✗ **Supply Chain and Consistency**

✗ **Manpower and Training**

✗ **Marketing for Each New Location**

Shakeer and Shinas, to their credit, **listened** when we told them,

📌 **"Opening outlets isn't the challenge. Keeping them profitable is."**

So, instead of **rushing**, we worked on **building a strong foundation first.**

🏛 Phase 1: The Systematisation Before Scaling

Before outlet #2 even launched, we focused on **three things:**

1. **SOPs for Everything**

   We created **Standard Operating Procedures (SOPs)** for:

   - Tea preparation (exact timings, temperatures, and ingredient ratios)

   - Customer service (how to greet, upsell, and handle complaints)

   - Hygiene standards (daily cleaning checklists, audits)

   - Order management (a simple system to track sales and inventory)

2. **Staff Training Model**

   A business that runs on **one founder's personal supervision isn't scalable.**

   - We set up a **2-week staff training programme** before launching the second outlet.

   - Every new staff member had to **shadow an experienced team** before being assigned solo shifts.

3. **A Strong Supply Chain**

One big mistake many food businesses make? **Not standardising their suppliers.**

- We helped them **negotiate bulk deals with suppliers** for tea leaves, *kulhads,* and packaging.

- This reduced raw material costs by **15%**, improving profit margins.

Once these systems were in place, **we launched outlets #2 and #3.**

☑ Phase 2: Expansion Without Burning Money

Between **year 1 and year** 3, Chai Junction went from **1 to 30+ outlets** without **losing control.**

How?

1. **The Franchise Model**

- Instead of using their capital for every outlet, they franchised the brand.

- Every franchisee had to **follow strict recipes, interiors, and service guidelines.**

- Franchise fee: ₹8-12 lakhs per outlet

- Franchise revenue: ₹2 crores in two years

2. **Location Strategy: Data-Driven, Not Emotional**

- No opening outlets based on gut feeling.

- Each location was chosen based on **footfall analysis, rental costs, and nearby competition.**

- **Prime spots:** Near colleges, IT parks, railway stations, and malls.

3. **Marketing That Created a Cult Following**

   - They didn't spend lakhs on **random ads.**

   - **Every outlet had a unique theme** (college chai spots, co-working chai zones, etc.).

   - Their **Instagram game was strong**—viral reels, influencer collaborations, and user-generated content.

   - **Community building:** They hosted **weekly chai meetups, open mic nights, and local artist showcases.**

💰 The Numbers That Proved It Worked

📊 **Year 1 (1 outlet):** ₹5 lakhs/month revenue, ₹50k profit/month

📊 **Year 2 (10 outlets):** ₹40 lakhs/month revenue, ₹6 lakhs profit/month

📊 **Year 3 (30 outlets):** ₹1.6 crores/month revenue, ₹25 lakhs profit/month

🔑 The Biggest Lessons From Chai Junction's Success

✅ **Grow Slowly But Strategically:** They didn't rush into expansion; they **built a strong base first.**

✅ **Systemise Early:** Without SOPs, **scaling leads to chaos.**

☑ **Leverage Franchising (If Done Right):** It gave them growth without huge capital risk.

☑ **Invest in Community, Not Just Ads:** Customer loyalty was built through engagement, not discounts.

✵ Where Are They Now?

Shakeer and Shinas are planning an **international expansion** with outlets in **Dubai and Malaysia.**

- ✦ Their model is so **well-structured** that they can launch a new outlet with **zero drop in quality.**

- ✦ They have a **dedicated training centre** for new franchise owners.

- ✦ Chai Junction is now a ₹**20 crore brand**—all because they scaled **the smart way.**

The Final Takeaway?

✵ Scaling is not about "how fast" you expand. It's about **how well you prepare for it.**

Most businesses fail in expansion because they don't systematise first.

Chai Junction's story proves that **growth is inevitable if you plan, structure, and execute correctly.**

End Note: The Consultant's Role and the Entrepreneur's Responsibility

This book is a collection of the most significant lessons I have gathered from my experience across 3,000+ consulting assignments. Many of these cases share similar challenges, yet each one reinforces a fundamental truth: a consultant can only bring meaningful transformation to an organisation when the entrepreneur takes ownership of the change process.

Over the years, I have witnessed first-hand how the success or failure of a consulting engagement largely depends on the mindset and leadership of the business owner. While a consultant provides the framework, strategy, and roadmap for growth, the entrepreneur ultimately must take the driver's seat and steer the organisation toward change. Hesitations, delays in decision-making, weak leadership, and the inability to transition from an "employee mindset" to a "leader's mindset" often hold back progress. Many business owners expect external interventions to work like magic, but real and lasting improvements require deep commitment, swift action, and a willingness to evolve.

A consultant is not a miracle worker but a guide, a strategist, and a catalyst for change. Success and stagnation differ in how well an entrepreneur applies the consultant's recommendations. The most remarkable transformations I have seen have come from business owners who took decisive action, embraced difficult but necessary changes, and led their teams with clarity and conviction.

If you are an entrepreneur reading this book, I urge you to reflect on your leadership approach. Are you truly prepared to take charge of your business transformation? Are you ready to make the tough calls, break old habits, and implement new systems? A consultant can walk the path with you, but the responsibility to act—and to drive the change—rests with you.

The business world rewards those who take action. Make sure you are one of them.

– AR RANJITH

9 798897 779222